W9-AAY-590

Praise for *The Worry Solution*

"In this accessible tome, [Dr. Martin Rossman] presents tried-and-true solutions . . . the good doc delivers what his title promises."
—*USA Today*

"Dr. Rossman turns worry upside-down and shows how it can actually be beneficial if handled wisely. *The Worry Solution* may be the last book on stress management you'll ever need to buy."
—Larry Dossey, M.D., author of *The Power of Premonitions*

"A unique marriage of timeless wisdom, cutting-edge brain science, and practical techniques that stop runaway worry and stress. *The Worry Solution* is first-rate medicine for your heart, your health, and your daily life."
—Dean Ornish, M.D., founder and president of the Preventive Medicine Research Institute, clinical professor of medicine, University of California, San Francisco, and author of *The Spectrum*

"*The Worry Solution* is a wonderful contribution to the age-old question of what to do about worry or anxiety. Marty Rossman is a pioneering contributor to integrative medicine. He knows the science and, as a practicing physician, he knows what actually works for real people. If worry is a problem in your life, I recommend *The Worry Solution* highly."
—Michael Lerner, Ph.D., president of Commonweal

"Profound lessons in a straightforward, pleasure-to-read format. No preaching, just the kind, considerate guidance of a very experienced physician teaching you how to let go of stress and enjoy life more."
—Kenneth R. Pelletier, Ph.D., M.D., clinical professor of medicine and professor of public health, University of Arizona and UCSF Schools of Medicine, and author of *The Best Alternative Medicine* and *New Medicine*

"*The Worry Solution* will teach you how to use your mind and brain to eliminate unnecessary suffering and the negative health impacts caused by worry." —Shirley MacLaine

"A marvelous, marvelous book! I am amazed that it is possible to become happier without changing anything in your outer life. *The Worry Solution* really worked for me and I bet it will work for you too!"
—Rachel Naomi Remen, M.D., author of *Kitchen Table Wisdom* and *My Grandfather's Blessings*

ALSO BY MARTIN ROSSMAN, M.D.

Fighting Cancer from Within: How to Use the Power of Your Mind for Healing

Guided Imagery for Self-Healing

THE
WORRY
SOLUTION

✺

USING YOUR HEALING MIND
TO TURN STRESS AND ANXIETY
INTO **BETTER HEALTH** AND **HAPPINESS**

✺

MARTIN ROSSMAN, M.D.

HARMONY

BOOKS · NEW YORK

Copyright © 2010 by Martin L. Rossman, M.D.

Published in the United States by Harmony Books, an imprint of the
Crown Publishing Group, a division of Penguin Random House LLC,
New York.
crownpublishing.com

Harmony Books is a registered trademark, and the Circle colophon is a
trademark of Penguin Random House LLC.

Originally published in hardcover in the United States by Crown
Archetype, an imprint of the Crown Publishing Group, a division of
Penguin Random House LLC, New York, in 2010. Subsequently published
in paperback in the United States by Three Rivers Press, a division of
Penguin Random House LLC, New York, in 2010.

Library of Congress Cataloging-in-Publication Data
Rossman, Martin L.
The worry solution : using your healing mind to turn stress and anxiety into
better health and happiness / Martin Rossman. —1st ed.
p. cm.
1. Stress management. 2. Affirmations. 3. Holistic medicine. I. Title.
RA785.R675 2010
616.9'8—dc22   2010026873

ISBN 978-0-307-71824-2
eBook ISBN 978-0-307-71825-9

Printed in the United States of America

20 19 18 17 16 15 14 13 12

First Harmony Books Edition

This book is dedicated to my grandparents,
Louis and Jesse Shapero and Daniel and Esther Temchin.
They had a lot to worry about, and they handled it with
courage and grace.

The premise of *The Worry Solution* is simple.

You are wiser, stronger, and more creative than you think.

By the end of this book, you will know that for yourself.

CONTENTS

For many years the focus of my work has been to educate people, including doctors, about how to support the body's natural healing abilities. Many of my recommendations concern lifestyle choices that we can make. Selecting wisely from the many foods we have available to us can make the difference between a long life filled with vitality or one shortened or hobbled by chronic illness. Choosing to be physically active every day can preserve your mobility, increase your energy, and reduce your risk for many chronic diseases, including the diseases of aging. Learning to manage stress is perhaps one of the most critical choices you can make in order to enjoy a healthy, productive life.

Managing stress has a lot to do with how we worry, and managing worry has a lot to do with where we focus our attention. While there are risks and dangers in life that require our attention and response, our worrying can become a destructive habit, often perpetuated by the endless onslaught of media news and our failure to recognize that there are off buttons on our televisions, our computers, and even our minds. Life also offers us beauty, grace, and wisdom, and when we pay attention to them, both our health and the quality of our experience improve.

Humans are the only animals that create stress with their own minds. Much of that stress, and the anxiety that accompanies it, is unnecessary. We can lessen it by learning to use our minds more skillfully.

In *The Worry Solution*, Dr. Rossman addresses a critical problem of modern life. He shows us how worrying is a valuable mental function, but one that can go awry if we let it run away with us. He explains how we can use our awareness to sort useful worry from futile worry, transform futile worry into positive thought and affirmation, and engage the silent wisdom of our emotional/intuitive brains to enhance our creativity and problem solving.

In my first book, *The Natural Mind*, I wrote about a different kind of intelligence that was being revealed by both the experimental drug taking of the late 1960s and the great interest in meditation and Eastern philosophies that soon followed. While many observers became preoccupied with the very real dangers of inappropriate drug use, what they missed was that these experiments were attempts to connect with a way of thinking that is natural to humans, a way nearly lost in modern Western culture. This more holistic, synthetic, intuitive, and emotional way of thinking expands our awareness and gives us a different and frequently very useful perspective on the challenges and opportunities we face in life. The meditation and relaxation techniques, and especially the guided imagery processes, that Dr. Rossman teaches in this book can provide safe access to the intuitive and relational wisdom inside us all, without the need for mind-altering substances, whether recreational or pharmaceutical.

Marty Rossman is one of the preeminent modern figures in mind/body medicine. Through his books, his CDs, and the professional training academy he cofounded, he has taught hundreds of thousands of health professionals and laypeople to use their imagination for increased personal awareness, self-healing, and greater enjoyment of life. Marty is one of the few experts I asked to be part of my executive planning committee when I created the Integrative Medicine Fellowship at the University of Arizona, and he and I co-created *Self-Healing with Guided Imagery*, the first in my series of educational self-care audio programs for the public. Because of his unique expertise about the importance of the mind in health and illness, I also invited him to write the mind/body medicine chapter in the recent *Integrative Oncology* textbook I coedited with Dr. Donald Abrams. He has a gift for making the healing and creative gifts of imagination immediately accessible and practically useful.

If you don't use your imagination skillfully, it can be hijacked by your fears, keeping you unnecessarily stuck in an inner world of anxiety and stress. Letting yourself fall into what Dr. Rossman calls the "bad worry" habit is like feeding junk food to your mind. Reclaiming control of your imagination can let you use its creativity, wisdom, and motivational power to solve problems and enjoy life more. I am happy to commend you to a masterful teacher who will teach you how to do just that.

—Andrew Weil, M.D.
Director, Integrative Medicine Program
University of Arizona Medical School

THE **WORRY** SOLUTION

I am a doctor. My mission, and my passion, is to stimulate healing in people, cure illness when I can, and relieve suffering when cure is not possible.

Worry is the most common form of suffering in America. It is a key component of anxiety and chronic stress, and is often at the heart of overeating, alcoholism, cigarette smoking, drug abuse, and other compulsive but ultimately ineffective attempts to make it go away.

Anxiety is one of the most uncomfortable feelings you can have, and much of it is triggered by a "bad worry" habit. You will find that this habit can be changed into a way of thinking that is not only more comfortable but much more productive, and that a great deal of your worry is optional and unnecessary.

In this book, I will teach you how to stop creating unnecessary suffering for yourself and others, and how to use worry for its true purpose, which is to keep you and your loved ones safe from harm.

The Worry Solution's program will teach you how to clarify your worries, sort them into those you can and cannot do anything about, and use the wisdom hidden in the large silent areas of your brain to help you solve real problems creatively. You will learn effective ways to shift from negative worry states into more positive frames of mind. You will also learn how to stop hypnotizing yourself with scary thoughts, and concentrate instead on thoughts that bring you creativity, courage, calmness, and confidence.

If we are going to worry—and let's face it, we are—we might as well learn to worry well. Let me show you how.

I. Wired to Worry

✳

We suffer more from imagination than from reality.
— SENECA

✳

Everybody worries sometimes, and many of us worry all the time. Worry helps us survive. It helps us avoid danger, or plan how best to respond to it. Humans alone are blessed (and cursed) with the ability to imagine and predict the future, which has made us both the most successful animal on earth and also the most troubled. The price we pay for being able to think about the future is to know that we are mortal, and to know that we are vulnerable. *Homo sapiens,* the "one who knows," could just as accurately be called the "one who worries."

Our imagination lets us turn a problem over and over in our minds, seeking the perspective that will let us resolve the situation. To worry is a bit like untangling a big ball of yarn. You find a little give here and a little loosening there, then you get stuck, so you turn it over and find a bit of room to move on the other side. If you keep at it, you will usually get it straightened out. Sometimes our most tangled life problems can also be resolved through a similar kind of worrying process.

Solving problems is the positive, healthy function of worry, but worry can easily turn into a bad habit of endless rumination about frightening, threatening, or simply annoying matters that ultimately cannot be solved. This kind of unskillful worrying can become a self-defeating form of self-suggestion that creates or amplifies anxiety and stress where none really needs to be.

If you had a prefrontal lobotomy, you wouldn't have much worry. A lobotomy is an extreme neurosurgical answer to mental illness, one that flowered in the early twentieth century, when other treatments for serious mental illness included insulin shock, shock therapy with cold wet blankets, and inducing malaria in patients. All of these were crude attempts to relieve the suffering of psychosis by "rebooting" brains gone wrong.

Neurosurgeons of the day performed lobotomies by driving an ice pick through the inner corner of the eye socket and waving it back and forth to destroy connections between the thinking and feeling parts of the brain. This grisly procedure was not infrequently performed in the patient's home, on the kitchen table. Patients who survived often had much less anxiety, but the price they paid included a loss of emotion, planning ability, and creativity. Fortunately, lobotomies are almost never performed these days, because of the development of antianxiety, antidepressant, and antipsychotic medications that can often relieve symptoms without destroying substantial chunks of the brain.

Medical and even occasional surgical interventions have their places in treating severe, intractable mental illness, but their downside risks are much too high a price to pay for simple worrying. I only bring them up because they show that altering the relationship between the thinking and emotional parts of the brain can and does relieve anxiety, stress, and worry. Instead of destroying or medicating brain pathways, however, we can learn to use them more consciously to better effect.

Our brain is wired to worry, but we can learn to worry less. We can also learn to be more effective when we do worry by using our brain to find and strengthen qualities that we need in order to change difficult situations or to cultivate acceptance of problems that are beyond our ability to solve. I will show you how we can use our mind and brain (and yes, there is a difference between the two) to calm ourselves, and to access wisdom, courage, creativity, and other personal qualities that will transform worry into confidence and effectiveness.

In order to make this transformation, we will use our imagination to add the wisdom of our unconscious emotional/intuitive mind to the conscious logic of our thinking mind. Worry, especially "bad" or futile worry, is simply imagination run amok. Using the imagination skillfully can not only eliminate unnecessary worry but also help us create the future we desire, and guide us wisely through life's difficult passages.

Melanie, a forty-three-year-old mother of two young children, was shocked when her husband, Paul, announced that he was leaving the family. When she discovered that another woman was involved, her shock was compounded by a nearly overwhelming mixture of rage, embarrassment, fear, and worry. Friends and family were very supportive and offered lots of advice, much of it conflicting. At times she felt like dying, and at other times she felt like she would go crazy, but she knew she had to stay strong for her children's sake. Fortunately, she had some experience with mental imagery as a way to receive insight and guidance from her unconscious mind. In the midst of all this stress, she took some time out to relax and asked her unconscious mind for an image that could help guide her through what she feared was going to be a long and terrible ordeal. An image of her about to paddle a kayak through very dangerous rapids came quickly to mind.

An accomplished and lifelong kayaker, she immediately understood that she was about to go through a passage that would demand all her skill and determination. In the same instant, she saw that while the effort would challenge her to the extreme, she could make it all the way through if she gave the challenge her full attention. She also got the sense that if she did make it through, she would be living life on a much deeper and more conscious level than she ever had before.

This image stayed with her throughout the many twists and turns of her divorce journey, reminding her to stay balanced while she focused on each turn. The image indicated that, like a kayaker, she needed to be aware of the dangers and obstacles in front of her, but she also needed not to become preoccupied with them. She knew that a paddler who stares at the rocks she doesn't want to hit is much more likely to hit them than a paddler who looks at the line between the rocks. When you run a fast river, you tend to go where you look, and Melanie got the message that the same principle applied to her life situation.

Melanie kept her eye on her goals, which were to protect herself and her children and to be able to love again. Melanie made it and is now happily remarried and thriving, and she often says that this simple image gave her constant reassurance that she would be able to handle whatever she needed to handle during this very stressful and unexpected life challenge. Melanie's intuitive brain, expressing itself through this exquisitely tailored image, gave her hope, direction, and focus in a time of fear, worry, and confusion. She not only understood but felt its message, which is one important reason that imagery can be so powerful—it is a mental language that can convey both reason and emotion.

Imagination is a powerful mental function, but it is a double-edged sword. Our imagination can help us solve problems or it can scare us silly, depending on how skillful we are with it. If Melanie had not known to go deeper than her fears and worries, they could have easily overwhelmed her. Instead, she was able to find encouragement and guidance from her own unconscious mind, expressed through her imagination.

The human imagination, like the mind itself, is invisible and often taken for granted, but it is one of the most powerful forces on earth. Imagination has allowed humans to overcome our prey-animal vulnerability to become the most dominant creature on the planet. Imagination allows us to remember and learn from our past, mentally experiment with possible futures, and avoid unnecessary dangers and problems.

Everything made by humans, from skyscrapers and computers to subprime mortgages and atomic weapons, started in someone's imagination. Our imagination, along with our will, can literally determine whether we survive or self-destruct. The essential problem is that most of us have never been taught how to use this powerful tool in our daily lives. Too often, the default position for the untrained imagination is driving ourselves crazy or worrying ourselves sick, because things that frighten us tend to get our attention first and foremost.

Fear First

There's a good reason that the brain tends to focus on the negative and fearful. Worry is related to the brain's most important function: to protect us from harm and keep us alive. While our brain has many other uses, all levels of the brain are constantly on guard for threats to survival. While we modern humans act like, and to some degree are, the most powerful animal of all, we are still prey animals underneath, cautious and vigilant, and highly dependent on one another for safety. That's why our emotional brains so closely monitor our relationships to our families, friends, and associates. Threats to our personal or social well-being, real or imagined, send danger signals down through the oldest, most primitive part of the brain, trumpeting alarm throughout the body, setting off the well-known fight-or-flight response.

This protective reaction activates a host of mental, physical, and emotional responses designed to help us survive an immediate threat to our lives. Unfortunately, the stress response in our bodies does not fire only in response to direct physical challenges. Threats these days are rarely jungle predators. They are more often the hassles and pressures inherent in everyday life—the people, challenges, everyday responsibilities, and worries that we carry in our minds. They also include an avalanche of frightening information piped in from the outside world by a seemingly endless number of media channels that operate as if their economic survival is based on making sure that we know about every bad thing that has happened or could happen anywhere in the world at any given moment.

It's easy to get scared. But letting fear run away with your imagination leads to a futile "bad worry" habit that can keep you chronically stressed and anxious. The good news is that because this kind of worry begins in our brains, we can learn to use our brains to eliminate it when it is not productive—or improve it so that it *is* productive. Unskillful worry and the stress and anxiety that accompany it are to a large degree optional. Using your imagination differently, on purpose, can quickly change the way you feel, and show you a healthy way out of unnecessary distress.

A First Experiment with Imagery

Let me invite you to do a simple experiment to see how your imagination can influence the way you feel.

Make sure you are in a safe, comfortable place where you can close your eyes for a few minutes. Focus on your body, as if your attention were a radar or sonar beam slowly scanning up and down, and notice if you feel any stress, tension, or discomfort anywhere in your body. On a scale of 0 to 10, where 0 is no tension and 10 is all the tension you can stand, where would you rate the tension level in your body right now?

Now imagine that you are camping in the woods. In the middle of the night you need to go to the bathroom, so you partially dress and shuffle off so you won't disturb anybody else. It's completely dark with no moon and it takes you a while to find a level place, but you finally are able to do what you need to do. The need attended to, you notice how really dark it is, and you start to carefully pick your way back to camp, reaching out with your extended arms so you don't bump into anything. You trip over tree roots and rocks and pick up a few scratches from unseen branches. After a while you feel that you've been walking too long and should have found your campsite already. It's cold and dark and you're kind of uncomfortable.

You start walking in another direction, and then after a while another, and you realize that you are lost. You quietly call out several times but nobody answers; finally you yell loudly but still get no response. The night is even darker and colder, and you feel very alone. As you wonder what to do next, the background noises of the forest suddenly go strangely quiet.

You hear something moving in the brush nearby. It sounds like something big, and it is heading toward you.

Now, stop for a minute and rescan your body. Where would you rank your tension level now, on that 0-to-10 scale?

Imagine that from the direction of the breaking twigs you hear your good friend call out your name. It's not a bear. You are safe. Notice if your tension goes away immediately or if there is some aftereffect that lingers for a little while.

I apologize for scaring you, but the point is that if you did get tense or scared, it's because you have a good imagination, and you can see how intimately it is connected to your body. I promise that I will *not* scare you anymore with any of the exercises in this book, so you can safely experiment with them without worrying about that. My purpose here was just to demonstrate how your imagination could stimulate change in your body and mind.

Now that you've had a taste of how you can scare yourself with imagery, let's see how you can use it to relax, a much more useful and pleasant skill.

Here's the simplest way I know to relax. You can read this imagery process and then focus on your own imagery, but it will be more effective if you have someone slowly read you the stressbuster imagery script, giving you time between each sentence to imagine the different things I mention. You can also

record the exercise so you can relax and listen to *i*
option is to go to www.worrysolution.com and down.
audios of this and the other Worry Solution processes that
have professionally recorded for you.

PREPARING FOR THE STRESSBUSTER EXPERIENCE

Put the phone on the answering machine, or let your cell
phone go to voice mail and turn off the ringer. Let people in
your household know not to interrupt you for twelve to fifteen
minutes unless there is a true emergency. Loosen any tight or
restrictive clothing or jewelry and let yourself get comfortable
in either a sitting or reclining position. Let any irrelevant outside noises go to the background of your awareness as you concentrate on the suggestions I will offer you.

Take a moment again to scan your body, and estimate how
much tension you feel on a scale of 0 to 10, where 0 is no tension at all and 10 is wired as tight as you can get.

STRESSBUSTER IMAGERY

Take a deep breath or two and let the out-breath be a "letting-go"
kind of breath. Invite your body to feel relaxed, like it's made out
of warm wet noodles. When you're ready, recall some place you've
been in your life where you felt safe, relaxed, and peaceful. If you
don't have such a place, perhaps you've seen one in a movie or a
magazine, or you can just imagine one right now.

Just let yourself begin to daydream that you are in a safe, beautiful, peaceful place...and let yourself notice what you imagine seeing
in this safe, beautiful place...what colors and shapes, what things you

---

see there. Don't worry about how vividly you see in your mind's eye, just notice what you imagine seeing and accept the way you imagine these things. In the same way, notice what you imagine hearing in that beautiful peaceful place, or is it very quiet? Just notice. Is there an aroma or a quality in the air that you notice? You may or may not and it doesn't really matter; just notice what you notice in this special peaceful place. Can you tell what time of day or night it is? Can you tell the season of the year? What's the temperature like?

Notice how it feels to be in this safe, beautiful, and peaceful place. Notice how your body feels, and how your face feels. Notice any sense of comfort or peacefulness or relaxation that you may feel there. Take some time to explore and find the spot where you feel most relaxed and at ease in this place, and just let yourself get comfortable there. Take a few minutes to just enjoy being there, with nothing else you need to do. If it feels good to you, imagine that you are soaking up the sense of peacefulness and calmness like a sponge; feeling more and more relaxed and at ease as you enjoy this place of calmness.

Take as long as you want, and when you are ready, let the images go, and gently bring your attention back to the outside world, but if you like, bring back any feeling of peacefulness or calmness that you may feel. When your attention is all the way back, gently stretch and open your eyes and look around, bringing back with you anything that seemed interesting or important, including any sense of calmness you may feel.

REVIEWING YOUR STRESSBUSTER EXPERIENCE

Notice how you feel as you come back to your outer world. When you are ready, scan your body again, and see where you would rank your tension on a scale from 0 to 10. Most people find that they feel calmer, more relaxed, and more peaceful after doing this simple kind of imagery. If this is true for you, notice that you shifted into this state simply by focusing your imagination on pleasant things that you imagined seeing, hearing, feeling, and perhaps smelling.

Your brain sent messages that were safe and relaxing, and your body responded accordingly, as it always tries to do.

Are Worry, Anxiety, and Stress All the Same?

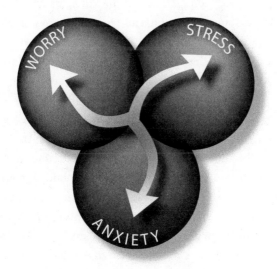

Worry, anxiety, and stress are so intricately interconnected that they can be confused or assumed to be the same. But they are different from one another, and understanding the differences is important for understanding how to use the Worry Solution model.

Worry is a type of *thinking* in which we turn knotty problems over and over in our minds. It helps us examine different angles and perspectives so that we can uncover solutions that are not immediately apparent. This is the "good" kind of worry. Unfortunately, worry can also become a destructive mental habit of repetitive, negative self-suggestion that creates stress and can lead to chronic anxiety and depression. Worry lives in the thinking part of the brain, behind the forehead, in certain areas of the prefrontal cortex, the most uniquely human part of the brain.

Anxiety, on the other hand, is an uncomfortable *feeling* of apprehension or dread. It's the "oh my God, something bad is going to happen" feeling. It lives in the limbic system, an evolutionarily older, more emotional and intuitive part of the brain. A person's tendency to be anxious depends on genes, early family life, gender, and life experiences. Women tend to have more anxiety than men, and people who have experienced trauma, especially early in life, tend to be more anxious than those that haven't. Their limbic brain actually rewires itself to be more vigilant than it was before the trauma occurred.

Stress, the third element in our uncomfortable triad, is a *physical response* to danger that prepares the body for survival in threatening circumstances. It is an instantaneous, unconscious reaction activated in the oldest, most primitive part of our brain, the part we call the reptilian brain. When the reptilian brain receives the danger signal either from the environment or from higher brain centers, it instantaneously relays that alarm throughout the body, and the resulting stress response physiologically prepares us to run or fight for our lives.

For our ancestors, when the danger was typically an attack by a predator or enemy, the outcome was either that they overcame the attacker, managed to escape, or were killed. If they survived the attack, they returned to their cave, told their story, then probably slept for a day or two while their bodies replenished the chemical stores they had used up during their intense survival response. Then they probably told the story again around the evening fire on frequent occasions, sharing what they had learned and, after a while, probably boring their listeners to sleep.

Modern Stress Is Different from Natural Stress

Modern stresses are different from the stresses of the wild. It's not that there aren't plenty of things to worry about, but for most of us in the developed world the predominant sources of stress are now *internal* rather than *external*. They have as much or more to do with what we think about than with what happens to us. Fortunately, we rarely encounter animals or people who want to eat or harm us. But the rapid pace of modern life creates a challenge unprecedented in previous human experience—dealing with the sheer volume of potentially threatening information we process each day.

According to a recent analysis done at the University of California, San Diego, the amount of information consumed by the American public in 2008 was 3.6 zettabytes, or the equivalent of a seven-foot-high stack of novels covering the entire United States, including Alaska. The average American receives data through television, Internet, radio, movies, computer games, and print media for nearly twelve hours a day! Just a small percentage of this information avalanche is more than the average pre-1900 human ever needed to process in his or her entire lifetime. It taxes our ability to sort it, separate the important from the trivial, and decide what, if anything, to do with it.

Even more taxing is that so much of the content of the news programs, documentaries, films, emails, and advertisements we are exposed to every day is alarming, frightening, or problematic. Fear sells news, entertainment, and many other products, from insurance policies to household cleaners to medications, because fearful information is hard for the brain to ignore. We are wired to pay priority attention to frightening information so that we can protect ourselves. If we were walking through the jungle and didn't go on high alert when we heard a rustle in the underbrush, we'd soon be lunch for some hungry predator.

Being tuned in to every signal that might be frightening makes sense in the wild, but we need a different mental strategy in an artificial, fear-laden media environment. We need a significant "software upgrade" in order to be able to cope with this huge amount of frightening but mostly irrelevant information. If we are running mental programs more suitable to a bygone era, the resulting anxiety or stress response can make it difficult to slow down or relax the brain to let it recover, renew, and refresh itself. A runaway imagination fueled by fear, information overload, stress hormones, caffeine, and the contagious anxiety of others not only creates tension during the day but can continue to work into the night, interfering with our sleep and pouring fuel on the fire of brain strain and exhaustion. The result is a burgeoning epidemic of worry, anxiety, and stress.

THE COST OF WORRY

It is commonly estimated that for both men and women, between 50 and 75 percent of all visits to primary-care doctors in the United States are intimately related to stress or unresolved emotional upset. Unrelieved stress is recognized as a significant risk factor for heart disease, stroke, high blood pressure, autoimmune disease, fibromyalgia, chronic pain syndromes, irritable bowel syndrome, insomnia, and asthma, among many other illnesses too numerous to name. Toxic and ineffective attempts to manage stress account for the United States being the most chemically dependent society ever to exist, with epidemic levels of obesity, alcoholism, and drug addiction in addition to the pandemic routine use of prescription and over-the-counter medications.

Over 20 percent of Americans (60 million people) have diagnosable anxiety disorders, which include generalized anxiety disorder, panic disorder, agoraphobia, specific phobias, post-traumatic stress disorder, and obsessive-compulsive disorder. These are two to three times as common in women. Another 60 to 100 million struggle with toxic habits or addictions ranging from alcoholism, cigarette smoking, and drug addiction to eating disorders. And almost everyone else is simply nervous about what's going on in the world and would like to find a way to feel more relaxed.

WHY WOMEN WORRY MORE

Women tend to be more anxious than men, especially once they've had children, for a variety of good reasons. Women are typically smaller, lighter, and more vulnerable than men, and their children are even more so. Being extra vigilant helps not only the individual woman but also her offspring (and hence the species) to survive. Female hormones actually alter a woman's brain to be especially sensitive to signs of threat and danger. Her amygdala and anterior cingulate gyrus, areas of the brain that are intimately involved with processing fear, anger, and analysis of emotional events, are several times larger than those of the average man.

Fortunately, women also tend to have an extra helping of emotional and intuitive intelligence, with significantly more of their brains devoted to emotional recognition, processing, and expression. Because emotional and intuitive thinking is undervalued in our culture, this remarkable power is rarely used as well as it might be.

Whatever your gender, *The Worry Solution* will teach you ways to use this special intelligence more skillfully and integrate it with the type of rational thinking we typically value more highly.

CAN WE CHANGE HOW MUCH WE WORRY?

Many chemicals, natural or man-made (including caffeine, alcohol, nicotine, tranquilizers, antidepressants, amino acids, and herbs), can increase or decrease the tendency to be anxious. The most exciting news, especially for people who want to avoid or can't tolerate chemicals, is that learning to think differently can also decrease anxiety and stress. The anxiety pathways in the brain are not only chemical-sensitive but also thought-sensitive. Changing the nature of the conversation between the thinking and feeling parts of the brain will significantly reduce worry and anxiety, and effective relax practices can markedly lower the reactivity level of the brain to stress.

The most exciting news is that during the last two decades, we have learned more about how the brain functions than in all the time that came before, largely because technologies such as SPECT and functional MRI (fMRI) scanning have allowed us to look at brain activity in real time. We can identify what parts of the brain are activated when we are performing various tasks or even thinking about performing tasks. We see that when you think about being physically active, the parts of your brain that control and support that activity get stimulated, and when you think about relaxing, other parts of the brain that support relaxation get activated. Most important, we see that the brain changes constantly, and that the brain can learn new patterns and pathways at almost any age. This phenomenon, called neuroplasticity, shows us that old dogs really can learn new tricks, and when we learn new tricks, our brains change along with our minds.

Brain scientists have shown that giving information to the brains of people born blind can allow the visual processing parts of the brain to develop vision good enough to let them walk around unfamiliar rooms without bumping into obstacles. A basic premise of *The Worry Solution* is that if the blind can learn to see, the worried can learn to relax.

WHY MOST WORRY IS OPTIONAL

Fortunately, what we need to make these changes resides right between our ears. Fear does capture our attention and trumps other input—at first. But then our cortical "thinking caps" give us an alternative to being stuck in fear, and that's the ability to use our higher brain centers to protect, calm, reassure, and to some degree reset the reactivity of the lower brain centers that are more instinctual and unconscious. We can learn to relax, shift focus, evaluate our thought patterns, and create new ones that work better; essentially, we can learn to worry less but more effectively than we did before.

Most of us have never been taught to use our imaginations skillfully or well. We get stuck in the default position, which is to worry needlessly, habitually, and ineffectually. It's not that there isn't plenty to worry about; it's just that some of it is optional and unnecessary. At this critical time in human history, when we are facing so many personal, social, and global challenges, it is imperative that we learn to use our brains to full capacity and not fritter away energy on futile worry.

The same mental faculty of imagination that underlies much of your worry, anxiety, and stress also provides the tools that can liberate you from the tyranny of the endlessly worried mind. Because you are conscious, you have the ability to observe, choose, and change your thoughts. If you change your thoughts enough, your brain changes, too.

If you want to, you can learn to worry less, but more effectively. You'll be happier and more relaxed when you learn to "worry well."

2. Worrying Well

*Men ought to know that from nothing else
but the brain come joys, delights, laughter,
and sports, and sorrows, grief, despondency,
and lamentations.*

—HIPPOCRATES

I come from a long line of good worriers, and you probably do, too. Our ancestors worried enough, and worried well enough, to survive and procreate. But our challenges are different from theirs because of the immense amount of frightening information available to us at all times. We need to use our minds even more skillfully than they did or risk being immobilized in an avalanche of anxiety.

The Worry Solution program will relieve you of a great deal of unnecessary worry and stress. If you work through the five basic skills I will teach you, I guarantee that you will be worrying less and solving problems more effectively when you do worry. The Worry Solution will have you using your brainpower to resolve life challenges instead of frittering it away on worries you can't do anything about.

In the chapters that follow, I will teach you ways to clarify your worries, sort them into those you can do something about and those you cannot, and learn to use the intelligence of not only your rational brain but also your emotional and intuitive brain to come to terms with each type. The "secret sauce" in the Worry Solution is learning to use imagery, the natural language of large parts of your brain that are often ignored or undervalued. Imagery-based thinking brings the intelligence of your emotional/intuitive brain online, to add to the logical intelligence you are already using. The ability to imagine is one of the most powerful human mental functions, but few of us have ever been taught to use it skillfully.

The human imagination is unique in the world. It lets us remember the past and mentally experiment with possible futures so that we learn from our mistakes. It gives us mobility in time as well as space. It allows us to symbolize our thoughts and feelings and to draw on our creativity. Imagination is also the source of most of our worry, creating anxiety and stress if we let it get out of control.

Fortunately, recent brain science findings, clinical research, and time-honored traditions all show us that we can learn to use our imagination, and the brain pathways that it uses, to replace worry and stress with calmness, curiosity, and creativity. We can learn to reset our arousal levels, stimulate creative problem solving, and learn from the wisdom of our emotional/intuitive brains. As we learn to use our brain capabilities in new ways, we build the confidence that comes from successfully meeting life's challenges.

Our Minds Can Change and So Can Our Brains

Medical diagnostic tools including fMRI, PET scanning, and EEG brain mapping have allowed us to see, in real time, what parts of the brain are working when we worry, anticipate problems, get anxious, and become stressed. Showing us how worry, stress, and anxiety are interconnected in the brain, these studies also reveal how specific ways of thinking can prevent or relieve these distressing conditions.

The most important discovery of the last few years is that at any age, and often in spite of serious brain injury or abnormality, people can change not only their mind but also their brain. Stroke victims given new stimuli through mirror images are now recovering function in paralyzed limbs years after their brain-damaging events. People with obsessive-compulsive thinking can learn new thinking patterns that change their brain chemistry and structure. Brain researchers have even been able to give eyesight to people born blind by translating visual input from a camera into electrical signals on their back or tongue. This neuroplasticity seems to be an ability that we have throughout our lifetime.

As I said before, if the blind can learn to see, then we who are anxious and stressed can learn to relax. For that matter, if an eight-week-old puppy can be housebroken, then we should be able to learn new ways to think, feel, and act.

The Worry Solution

The Worry Solution program is a whole-brain, whole-person approach. It has a rationale and structure, and a series of skills and practices that let you put it to immediate practical use.

The first step in the program will be to sort your worries into those you might be able to resolve through action and those that you cannot. Then you will learn a way to enhance your creativity and problem-solving abilities so that you can be more effective in resolving the issues you can change, and other methods that will help you come to terms with those that you cannot change. If you aren't sure whether a worry is solvable or not, I will teach you a practice that will connect you with a source of wisdom you may not know you have.

You might recognize this program foundation in the well-known Serenity Prayer: "Lord, grant me the serenity to accept those things I cannot change, the courage to change the things I can change, and the wisdom to know the difference." While the Serenity Prayer is often identified with twelve-step recovery programs, it is an old prayer; a form of it appears in ancient Roman texts. It was popularized in modern times by a theologian named Reinhold Niebuhr, who had it printed on cards and distributed to U.S. troops during World War II. Whatever its origin, the Serenity Prayer is a perfect framework for learning to worry well. If you are not a religious or spiritually oriented person, simply omit the word *Lord* and use it as a practical way to think about dealing with worry.

There are only two options when a situation is worrying you: change the situation or change your reaction. Of course, a third option is to continue to worry as you are doing now, but you wouldn't be reading this book if that was working for you.

While the Serenity Prayer gives us a structure for clarifying our worries, specific guided imagery practices will add depth and brainpower to your ability to change either yourself or your situation, and to wisely tell the difference.

Wisdom is something that typically comes with age and experience, and you might think that you cannot suddenly become wiser than you are. I would argue that when you are worried, anxious, and stressed, you may not be using the wisdom you already have. A relaxation and guided imagery technique will frequently reconnect you with your own wisdom in a very short period of time.

Amy was a forty-eight-year-old mother of three who felt she was coming apart because of the many stresses in her life, none of which she felt she was handling well. Her children and their many activities demanded huge amounts of her time. Her mother, nearing eighty and living thousands of miles away, was showing signs of dementia, and her brother and sister, who lived close to their mom, thought that she needed to move out of her longtime home into a senior housing facility. Amy's mother was ambivalent at best and distressed about not knowing what to do. Amy was going to visit frequently, taking red-eye flights for two-to-three-day weekend visits, and was both exhausted and terribly torn about what to do.

In a session with me, Amy said, "There is no good solution—no matter what I do, I feel guilty. I want to do the best I can for my mom, but I can't figure out what I can do and what I can't. My kids need me more than I can be available, and my husband and I rarely have any time together. I stay up late trying to get things done, I can't sleep through the night, and my moods are swinging all over the place. How long can I go on like this? It's like torture. I feel like I'm going to explode."

I suggested that we do a guided imagery session. After leading Amy through a relaxation process, I invited her to imagine that she was in a safe, comfortable place and then ask her unconscious mind for an image that represented the wisest, most loving part of herself. As she relaxed she imagined herself at a lake where she used to vacation with her family as a child. She imagined sitting on the dock in the sun, the warmth of the sun on her face, and looking out over the calm surface of the beautiful lake.

When she mentally requested a wisdom figure to join her, an image of her mother appeared, as young as she must have been when they spent those summers at the lake. In Amy's imagination, her mother was calm and loving and held a basket of freshly picked blackberries. Amy cried as she imagined eating the sweet blackberries with her mother, with her mother's comforting arm around her. I encouraged Amy to tell the image of her mother what was troubling her and how she felt about it all. Tears quietly fell from Amy's eyes, and when she was finished, I asked her to let the image respond to her in a way she could understand. In her mind's eye, her mother held her and told her that things seemed so much more complicated now, with so many more choices than there used to be. Her mother said that these things were hard for her generation, too, but when people got old, their families would just take care of them; there were no other options. Kids just did their homework and played outside with their friends on the street when they were done. There was more time to think and more time to feel, and people socialized in a more leisurely way.

As Amy listened, she saw how compressed her life had become, with tightly scheduled meetings, kids' activities, hurried visits to her mother, and lots of pressure to make decisions quickly and get an endless to-do list done. She saw that she couldn't do anything about her mother's aging, but that she did have some choices that could affect the quality of the remaining time they had together. She also realized her kids needed to understand how important it was for families to care for each other, no matter what the circumstances. When she imagined talking to her kids about this, she imagined that they understood and responded positively.

When I saw Amy three weeks later, she was much more relaxed. She had talked with her husband and her children and they all agreed that everybody's schedule was too tightly packed.

They trimmed their schedules and prioritized to make time for more family activities. Amy and her husband set a date night once a week, which they hadn't done for years.

Amy told me that our imagery session helped her realize that an important family decision such as the one regarding her mother could not be reduced to one more item on an overpacked to-do list. She called her brother and sister, and they agreed to rent a cottage for ten days up at the lake they had enjoyed as children. They would take their families and their mother, and show her how much they appreciated her. In that relaxed and loving atmosphere they would talk about what the best course would be for the future.

While Amy understood that the trip would be very emotional, she said, "At least we'll be doing it together, and even if we can't change what happens, maybe we can change the way we deal with it."

Amy used imagery to help her relax, and imagined having a conversation with a wise loving figure about an important and difficult issue. The imagery allowed her emotional intelligence to contribute its critical perspective to addressing this situation that had important ramifications for three generations of her family. What she learned helped her take the most appropriate actions in regard to her mother's condition, and also helped her better accept what she couldn't change. Her inner wisdom reminded her that relaxed family time was an invaluable resource that could help all of them with this difficult state of affairs.

The insight that led to this life-enhancing realization came in about twenty minutes, once Amy redirected her attention and invited her inner wisdom to come to mind. Too often we don't know or don't remember that we have this kind of wisdom within us, especially when we are anxious.

Amy's example shows us that imagery is a surprisingly effective way to shift mental gears in order to connect with wisdom that we may have lost touch with in our stressful state. Because imagery is a language that accesses areas of our brain different from the ones that think in words and numbers, it can open neglected channels of information and perspective. Relaxation and guided imagery have the ability to help us quickly shift states of mind so that we can effectively become almost instantaneously wiser than we thought we were.

No matter how wise we are, there are some worries and stressful situations that we cannot resolve. The Swiss psychiatrist Carl Jung once said, "The great problems of life are mostly unsolvable and must be lived through." With issues that must be accepted and lived through, imagery can connect us to other qualities, such as calmness, serenity, equanimity, humor, and compassion, that can make them more acceptable or at least more endurable.

THE COMPUTER ANALOGY AND THE WORRY SOLUTION MODEL

I was fortunate to teach at a brain/mind seminar with Dr. Daniel Amen, a brilliant psychiatrist who has pioneered the use of brain scanning to help diagnose and treat anxiety, depression, ADD, and other mental/emotional conditions. His many books, listed in the Resources section, are invaluable for people who suffer from these problems, and for us who are looking to worry less as well. As we chatted about our topics, Dr. Amen said, "I'm teaching about the hardware, and you're teaching about the software. It's important to address both."

If we imagine the brain as the hardware and the mind as

the software of consciousness, using imagery would be like taking an old computer, adding a thousand times the memory, and upgrading to an operating system that connects it to the Internet and lets it process information at a blazing rate. Because imagery is the natural coding language of most of the unconscious mind, representing large areas of the brain that are often kept silent, it adds a whole new world of information, problem-solving ability, and emotional intelligence to the intelligence you already have. It makes more brain resources available and exponentially expands your ability to deal successfully with worry and stress.

The diagram below illustrates the Worry Solution model. We clarify and sort our worries, address them with all of the ordinary intelligence we have, and then add the wisdom that

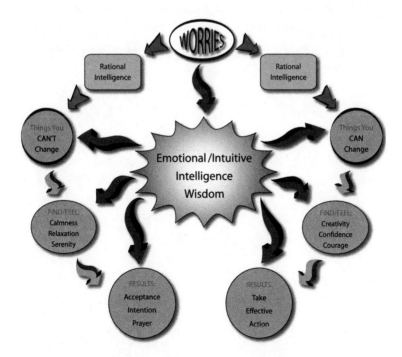

resides in our emotional and intuitive brains so that we can let go of what needs to be released and effectively change what needs to be changed.

Now that you understand the structure of the program, you can begin to explore the practices, which are where the benefits really reside.

Before you start, however, you may want to start a journal or log of your Worry Solution progress. It is very useful to track where you have been and what you learn from each experience. You can record your goals, experiences, insights, successes, challenges, and questions as you experiment with each technique, review your progress periodically, and keep track of other resources that you find helpful. You can make note of positive changes that you notice, and also areas that still need more attention. A journal or scrapbook for a program like this is a great learning tool. Make it attractive to you and keep it nearby as you work through the program and learn how to worry better.

3. Cultivating Calmness

✳

Anxiety is the dizziness of freedom.
—SØREN KIERKEGAARD

✳

Stress has become the medium in which we live our modern lives. Stress is the physical response we have to threatening thoughts and events—it's what happens when the brain fires the alarm signal and the body prepares to defend itself. Because there are relatively few imminent physical threats to our lives and well-being, most of the alarm signals that we send down our nervous system pipeline are provoked by our own thoughts and worries, and the fearful thoughts and worries of others. Our media keeps us very well informed of all the bad things that have happened or could happen all over the world, all the time. How we handle this massive information flow has a lot to do with how much time we spend stewing in our own stress juices.

Life is full of stress, especially for good worriers. Talented worrywarts ruminate over situations that cannot be resolved, stimulating an ongoing stress response where none needs to be. When we are highly stressed, the emotional brain gets aroused, which in turn stimulates the thinking brain to work harder to resolve our concerns. We create a vicious cycle where the baseline brain activity is geared to a higher than normal level, with increasing vigilance, fear, stress, and anxiety. Over time this extra effort depletes our energy, our ability to cope, and ultimately our self-confidence.

Stress as an important determinant of health has been a subject of medical scrutiny for some time. Harvard physiologist Walter Cannon first described the fight-or-flight response in the 1930s. Dr. Hans Selye at McGill University went on to describe the effects of longer-term stress responses shortly afterward, finding that chronically stressed laboratory animals developed a characteristic pattern in their little bodies: they developed stomach ulcers, their adrenal glands grew four to five times larger than usual from secreting so much adrenaline, and their lymph nodes and other immune-cell-producing tissues withered away.

Dr. Selye noticed that the initial response to chronic stress is a typical fight-or-flight arousal response, followed by a period he called "resistance," in which the stressed animal (or human) copes successfully with the ongoing stress. If the stress is unrelieved, however, it is eventually followed by a state of exhaustion and physical collapse. We primary-care doctors see this in our clinics all the time.

It is commonly said that 50 to 75 percent of all visits to primary-care doctors are for symptoms and illnesses directly attributable to the effects of stress. Chronic stress can cause not only anxiety, depression, and insomnia but also headaches, neck and back pain, indigestion, irritable bowel syndrome, high blood pressure, heart palpitations, trouble breathing, and a host of other physical symptoms. I can make the case that virtually every illness is stress-related because it is either caused by stress, aggravated by stress, or in itself is stressful. A great deal of a primary-care doctor's job is to try to determine if there is another type of illness hiding between the stress-induced symptoms.

Since Selye's discovery there has been a huge amount of research done on the effects of stress on mental health, physical health, and quality of life. We have learned to blame stress for a wide variety of symptoms and illness, but there is another factor involved that may be even more important: how we manage the stress we have.

Healthy, effective stress management includes physical exercise, talking things over with friends, family, or professional counselors, taking vacations, pursuing hobbies, praying, meditating, solving problems, and practicing relaxation techniques like the ones I will teach you. Excessive consumption of alcohol, overeating, smoking, and prescription or recreational drug use help to relieve stress in the short run but are toxic in the longer run. They are ultimately ineffective because they don't address the true nature of our stress or how we can best respond to it. They have adverse effects on our health and, most important, don't teach us how to cope.

Coping Is the Key

Not everyone experiencing the same stressful challenges gets sick or overcome by worry and anxiety. Psychologists Richard

Lazarus and Susan Folkman of the University of California, Berkeley, and the University of California, San Francisco, were the first stress researchers to shift their focus from stress to coping, which they defined as "efforts to master . . . demands that are appraised as taxing or exceeding the resources of the organism."

One of Dr. Lazarus and Dr. Folkman's key contributions to our understanding of stress was to recognize that the effects of stress could be tempered or amplified by our assessment of the situation and our abilities to deal with it. The effects of a stressful challenge are not simply a result of the challenge itself; they also greatly depend on our responses.

In the early 1980s the world's biggest company, AT&T, fell apart due to a change in regulatory laws. Hundreds of thousands of people were suddenly out of work or uncertain of their financial and career futures. Seven percent of the laid-off executives died within a year of this event, and many others fell ill with stress-related responses.

Suzanne Kobasa, a psychologist at the University of Chicago, studied the effects of this uncontrolled human stress experiment and noticed that there was a cadre of executives who, rather than collapsing under the weight of this stress, seemed to thrive during and after the corporate dismantling. Her now famous study identified characteristic traits in these people that she came to call the "three Cs": challenge, control, and commitment. When faced with a big change, these "stress-hardy" individuals responded to it as a challenge; they felt that they could have some control over what happened to them; and they felt committed to making the best of it, for their sake and that of others. Their response to stress protected them from adverse physical reactions. This may not be the only successful coping mechanism, but it dramatically demonstrates that how we respond to stress makes a huge difference in how it affects us.

Our coping responses are generally learned, and they are frequently not as effective as they could be. The great thing is, we can continue to learn, and we can become much more stress-hardy by learning to worry better.

How Do I Begin?

I am going to teach you five mental techniques that will help you let go of worry when it is useless and be more effective with worry when you are solving problems. You will find that each technique has its own particular strengths and benefits. When you have learned each of these skills, you will have a set of mental-emotional tools that can change your life for the better and transform you from a worrywart to a "worry warrior."

If I were going to teach you how to remodel a house, you'd first need to learn some basic carpentry skills, and would need to be able to use tools such as measuring tapes, hammers, saws, and levels. But once you started the job, the measuring, cutting, and nailing wouldn't all happen at once. You'd reach into your toolbox for the proper tool at the proper time, according to what was needed.

Worrying well is best approached the same way. First you'll learn and practice each skill and understand when and how to use it. As you experiment, you'll soon learn to apply these skills together or separately as each situation demands.

The Worry Solution involves using your whole brain. It draws on both traditional as well as emotional and intuitive thinking methods accessed through guided imagery. Reading this book and practicing the guided imagery exercises will help your thinking and feeling brains work better together.

The best way to use the guided imagery methods is to listen to recordings or readings of the exercises, so you can close your eyes and immerse yourself in the imagery. I have included scripts for each exercise so that you can record the scripts yourself or have someone read them to you. To make it even easier, I have professionally recorded all the exercises in this book to serve as practice guides as you get more familiar with each process. You can purchase these audios at www.worrysolution.com.

RELAXING THE BODY AND CALMING THE MIND

Learning to calm yourself and to deeply relax your mind, brain, and body is an essential skill if you are to learn to worry well.

Physical relaxation is important for many reasons. When we are responding to worry, the brain and body are preparing for action and using up nutrients at a high rate to stay alert. When we relax, our brains and bodies automatically repair, refresh, and renew themselves, replenishing depleted nutrients and strengthening our ability to cope.

Next, mental relaxation breaks the bad habit of automatically focusing on scary or worrisome thoughts and teaches you to shift your focus to calming, soothing, and comforting thoughts.

Third, deep relaxation allows you to view a familiar situation from a different perspective that may reveal new possibilities.

Fourth, learning to relax relieves feelings of helplessness because you'll find that there is almost always something you can do, at least internally, about almost any situation.

Finally, learning to relax puts you in a state of calm awareness in which you are more open to receiving helpful information and wisdom from parts of your brain that may be difficult to reach when you are busily engaged with the outside world. Learning to relax is fundamental to mastering the more complex skills I will teach you later.

Why Wouldn't We Want to Relax?

Anxious people are sometimes reluctant to try relaxation techniques because they are afraid of losing control. But realistically, how much control do you have if you can't ever relax? Learning to relax body and mind actually gives you *more* control, at least over yourself, no matter what situation you encounter.

Some people unconsciously resist relaxation because they have become conditioned or even addicted to their stress responses. We can easily fall into a vicious circle that starts with a bad worry habit leading to higher levels of vigilance, creating ongoing fight-or-flight responses and increased levels of physical arousal and sensitivity, which in turn stimulate even more worry. The catecholamine stress hormones (adrenaline and noradrenaline) released by our adrenal glands when we are under stress are stimulants that make us feel more powerful and effective, at least for a while. Any short-acting stimulant, whether cocaine, amphetamines, caffeine, or our own adrenaline, can become addictive, because it makes us feel smarter and more powerful for a while. When those effects fade away, we want to experience it again. Once we unconsciously discover that adrenaline stimulation is pleasurable, there are many ways to get a fix.

For instance, if you get a headache, you can imagine that it is a brain tumor. Sneezing and congestion? Probably a fatal case of influenza, or maybe a return of the bubonic plague. Overfill your schedule so that you are always running late. Bite off more than you can chew on a regular basis so that normal activities become frantic. Exaggerate the consequences of not getting everything done. Bring a sense of competition to everything you do, and constantly strive to be not only the best but perfect. Take everything personally. Keep a news channel playing in the background whenever you are awake, and consider leaving it on at night while you are trying to sleep. Always imagine the worst outcome in any situation. That should give you an ample supply of adrenaline—until, of course, your adrenal glands get exhausted, and you mentally or physically break down.

People who have become addicted to stress need to create stressful situations. They become drama queens (or kings) and create crises and chaos wherever they go. They amplify dangers and immediately imagine things going to their worst possible conclusions. They tend to approach life through a "sky is falling" mentality, turning small events into impending catastrophes.

If this is you, the Worry Solution will help you change this pattern. If you aren't this extreme in your responses, it'll help you even more. You'll have to get used to being calmer, having a bit less drama in your life, and finding other ways to relate to yourself and others, but you may be surprised at how quickly you adjust.

Another barrier to relaxation is a condition called "relaxation-induced anxiety." Approximately 10 to 15 percent of people get more anxious as they close their eyes and begin to relax. This is usually, though not always, due to some prior trauma. If this describes you, you may be able to overcome the problem by simply keeping your eyes open or half open so you can monitor the environment while you learn to relax. Or you might find that you can relax better if you have someone that you trust in the room. If these measures do not work, you may do best with the assistance of a well-trained health professional trained in this approach. See the Resources section or go to www.worrysolution.com for links to appropriate professionals.

Can We Really Change Old Patterns?

It seems to me that people change in one of two ways. Sometimes it happens in an instant, through a sudden insight, a crisis, or an epiphany. At other times change comes about only through regular practice over a long period of time. The Worry Solution practices create lots of opportunities for epiphanies by taking us into deeply relaxed and receptive states that make meaningful insights more accessible. Even if an epiphany doesn't occur, we are still practicing methods that that can change our brains over time. With regular repetition of these practices, we can become more "hardwired" for calmness and clarity rather than arousal and anxiety.

The Three Keys to Calmness

Cultivating calmness means that you must learn to operate three major "dual-control" mechanisms. These are built-in functions that operate automatically and unconsciously, but that can be used consciously as well.

The First Key to Calmness: Breath

I never imagined when I went to medical school how much time I was going to spend simply teaching many of my patients how to breathe. Not that they wouldn't breathe enough to keep them alive—that's automatic. But an interesting thing happens when we are stressed, tense, or anxious: our breathing gets shallow, and high in the chest.

This reaction is undoubtedly a throwback to our heritage as prey animals. Like rabbits or deer, if we sense a threat, we instinctively freeze, or go into a "still reaction" where we move as little as possible. Predatory animals such as lions, tigers, and wolves have eyes specifically designed to react to movement. The flight of a prey animal triggers them to give chase. The still response is the prey animal's defense. If there is no movement, the predator may not be able to see it, even if it is very close.

The problem with this still reaction in us modern humans is that most of the time there is no predator, so the reaction is pointless, and shallow breathing reduces our oxygen intake and increases our accumulation of carbon dioxide. These physiologic changes themselves, if unrelieved over time, trigger alarms in the body. So another repetitive cycle can become established, where stress responses induce shallow breathing, and shallow breathing leads to more stress and anxiety.

Fortunately, there is a simple fix, and it's one of your major tools against stress, tension, and anxiety. Breathing is a "dual control" mechanism. You will always breathe enough to maintain life, but you can also take conscious control of your breathing patterns, shifting from a stress response to a relaxation response and thereby breaking the pattern.

Belly Breathing

Here is a simple breathing experiment. The goal is to learn how to breathe using your abdomen, letting your belly move and even stick out when you inhale. Many people call this "belly breathing," though technically it's called "diaphragmatic breathing" because we use the diaphragm, the large muscle that separates the abdomen from the chest, to expand the chest and draw the breath deeper into the lungs. This deeper, more relaxed breathing not only improves our oxygenation and energy but also eliminates waste products and switches on the parasympathetic (or relaxation response) part of our autonomic nervous system. This is the part that takes over when our bodies are operating in the "all clear, no worries" mode they are meant to be in most of the time.

The simplest way to learn abdominal breathing is to use a method we use to teach it to children; it's called "balloon breathing." Lie on your back if that is comfortable, or if not, you can do this lying on one side or even sitting. Place one hand on your chest and one on your abdomen and just notice which hand moves more when you breathe normally. Don't try to change anything at this point; just notice which hand moves first as you inhale and which one finishes up the breath. If your chest hand moves first, see what happens if you consciously start the breath with the abdomen. Imagine that there is a balloon in your belly and that when you breathe, you expand the balloon and draw the breath directly into it. This may be awkward at first, but take a few minutes and experiment with it until you can start the breath by letting it come into the "balloon" and let your tummy expand. You may want to loosen any tight or restrictive clothing, belt, or undergarments while you learn to let the belly start the breathing. When you release your breath, imagine that the air is being released from the balloon in your belly and let yourself relax.

When you belly-breathe, your diaphragm muscles contract first, drawing the bottoms of your lungs down and pushing your belly out. This brings more breath into your lungs, improves the oxygenation of your blood, provides more energy, releases more carbon dioxide waste on the exhalation, and also gives you a gentle spinal massage as your spine moves rhythmically with the increased movement. Belly breathing triggers a relaxation response, and your whole system shifts into "clean up, fix up" mode. With no need to marshal forces to defend against external dangers or stresses, the body's innate repair and renewal systems can work at their unhindered best.

Yoga practices built on thousands of years of experience with balancing the body and mind emphasize the importance of the breath. The yogic science of breath (called *pranayama*) can teach us some patterns of breathing that are calming, and others that are energizing. The patterns that are calming tend to concentrate on drawing the breath into the abdomen, making your exhalation longer than your inhalation, and pausing at both the end of the in-breath and the out-breath.

Silently counting as you breathe in, pause, breathe out, and pause again will help you find a pattern that is easy and calming. Try inhaling on a count of four, pausing for a count of two at the end of the breath, exhaling on a count of six, and holding the breath out for a count of two, but feel free to vary the pattern until you find what works best for you.

Here's another experiment you can do with the relaxing abdominal breath. Get comfortable and loosen any tight clothing. Do this in a comfortable place where you won't be interrupted or bothered for five to ten minutes. To begin, scan your body slowly with your mind and rate the level of tension or stress you feel on an imaginary scale of 0 to 10, where 0 is no stress or tension at all and 10 is maximum stress and tension.

With one hand on your chest and one on your belly "balloon," let yourself breathe into your belly for a count of four, then hold it for a count of two. Exhale on a count of six or eight, whichever feels most natural to you, aiming to fully exhale all the air in your lungs, and then hold your breath out for a count of two. Do this for four breath cycles, then let your breath return to your normal rate and rhythm. Tune in and scan your body again, and rate your level of tension or stress now. Is it the same, lower, or higher than before?

If you are new to this type of breathing, it's possible that you might even get a bit more tense at first, because it can be awkward until you get into a rhythm that feels comfortable to you. Take your time and play with the breath, but aim to have the out-breath be longer than the in-breath, and pause at the end of each, just noticing the still point between each movement.

Once you feel more comfortable with the belly breath, try another series of six of them, then let your breathing go automatic and reassess your tension level. Notice if your stress and tension level is going down. If it is, repeat the six-breath cycle a few times, noticing how your body and mind responds to each cycle. If your tension level is not going down, leave this exercise alone for now and move on to the next one.

Reviewing Your Belly-Breathing Experience

Here are some things to think about as you review your experience. You may want to take some time to write in your Worry Solution journal, recording your responses to questions below or whatever you thought was interesting or important.

> What did you notice about your natural breathing patterns?
> What moved first when you started—your chest or your abdomen?

Were you able to change this sequence?

If so, what did you notice as you learned to breathe from the abdomen?

Was your breathing deeper? Did you find it relaxing after you got used to it?

Did anything get in the way?

Is there anything you can do about that so you can learn to belly-breathe more comfortably?

What happened to your tension levels as you practiced belly breathing?

Do you think you could breathe from your abdomen as you sit or stand? How about when you are walking?

Is this a technique you can use to help you be more relaxed if you want to?

Do you have any questions or comments about belly breathing and how it can help your mind and body begin to relax?

Don't forget, there are answers to frequently asked questions (FAQs) and other support materials available at www .worrysolution.com.

The Second Key to Calmness: Muscle Relaxation

The second "dual control" mechanism for relaxation is your level of muscle tension. Our muscles have a tension set point that automatically maintains their length and tension level. Some people have naturally loose muscles and some have naturally tight muscles. This can be altered to some degree with exercise or stretching, and you may be surprised to find that muscles also respond quickly to your thoughts and mental instructions.

We often maintain tension levels that are greater than we need, just from habit. When muscles are tense, their circulation is decreased and they tend to accumulate metabolic waste products such as lactic acid. Lactic acid is the substance that makes your muscles sore a day or two after you exercise more than usual. Besides making you sore, lactic acid also contributes to tension and stress. It is actually given by injection to human research subjects in order to stimulate anxiety!

Fortunately, your muscles rid themselves of lactic acid much more efficiently when you relax. In fact, your muscles clear lactic acid more than four times faster in a relaxed state than they do when you are asleep. An effective relaxation technique like the next one I will teach you can interrupt the pattern of muscle tension, lactic acid buildup, and increasing tension.

Besides noticing the relaxing effects of the breath, yoga practitioners have long recognized the fact that we can relax our muscles with our thoughts, and the invention of a device called the electromyograph (EMG) in the 1930s offered scientific confirmation of this. The EMG shows when muscles are receiving electrical signals from the brain. The same nerves that tell the muscle to contract can also tell the muscle to relax.

Edmund Jacobson, M.D., was one of the first EMG researchers. Dr. Jacobson asked people to imagine walking, running, or chewing while they were hooked up to the EMG. He found that when people imagined running their brains sent nerve impulses to the leg muscles, even though they didn't move; if they imagined eating a sandwich, they activated their jaw muscles. Their muscles were being "preheated" by their imaginations.

Dr. Jacobson found that when people suggested to themselves that their muscles relax, their muscles did in fact relax, creating an overall feeling of relaxation that seemed to be the opposite of the stress response.

When Jacobson taught his patients to relax this way, they

experienced relief not only from muscle tension and soreness but also from a wide variety of other physical and emotional symptoms. He wrote a popular book entitled *You Must Relax*, emphasizing how critically important it is to know that the body can react not only to suggestions that create fear or anxiety but also to those that create calmness and relaxation.

Dr. Jacobson called his method progressive muscular relaxation, and variations of it remain fundamental to anyone wanting to reduce stress and anxiety in the body and/or mind. It is known in yoga as *savasana* or corpse pose, which is usually done at the end of a session in order to let the body deeply relax. Muscle relaxation is also the primary content of the body scan often taught as a beginning mindfulness meditation practice, and the EMG remains an important tool used by biofeedback therapists to help people quickly learn to relax their muscles.

Muscle relaxation begins with scanning the muscle groups of your body in a gentle way and simply inviting them to relax. This calming practice not only releases built-up waste products that create pain and tension but also brings your attention to the present moment and away from your runaway imagination. It enhances your mind/body awareness and will also boost your sense of self-control as you sense your body responding to your thoughts.

The Third Key to Calmness: Calming Imagery

Mental imagery is the third key to relaxing the mind and reducing chronic stress and anxiety. The guided imagery practice of daydreaming yourself to a place that is beautiful, peaceful, and safe is an extremely effective way to shift out of your usual mind-set into one that allows your brain, body, and mind to deeply relax, renew, and replenish themselves. It can give you a refreshing respite and way to recharge during your day. In this simple Peaceful Place exercise, you may imagine going to a place you have actually visited, or to an imaginary place that comes to your mind; either is fine. The key to using this for deep relaxation is to pay close attention to all the sensory details.

As I mentioned earlier, a type of brain scan called a functional MRI can show us which parts of the brain are active when we are doing or even thinking about various things. The fMRI research reveals that as you imagine visual details, the area of your brain that does visual processing becomes active, and as you imagine the sound of the breeze in the trees, of ocean waves, or even of the quiet in your peaceful place, the part of your brain that processes hearing goes to work. So as you go through each sense (noticing odors, temperatures, time of day, and so on), more and more of your cortical brain gets involved in imagining a place of inner calmness and peace. As your cortex sends messages to your emotional and reptilian brains that you are relaxing in a safe, peaceful place, they issue the "all clear" relaxation signal to your body. As you focus on your senses in this pleasant way, you will find that your body and mind sink into a profound and renewing state of relaxation and calm.

The script that follows will lead you through a relaxation process that combines the belly breathing you learned with a muscle relaxation process followed by an inner journey to your own personal place of peace and comfort.

These three approaches work together to calm and reset your tension and arousal levels. This method of relaxing is easy, refreshing, empowering, and always available. At first it will take you about twenty-five minutes, but as you develop experience and confidence in your ability to relax you will be able to relax more quickly and easily, benefiting from the experience in just a few minutes.

Experiment with this method at least once and preferably twice a day for the next week and see how you feel. As with any learned skill, the more you practice, especially early on, the better you will get. Regular relaxation will help you feel better, relieve stress, and will also help you become more aware of what triggers tension in you.

Preparing for Deep Relaxation

For your own safety do *not* listen to any of these relaxation and guided imagery methods if you are driving or engaged in any other activity that requires your full attention. If possible, listen in a place that is quiet, comfortable, and safe, and ask others to not interrupt you unless there is a true emergency (which doesn't include helping them find their socks or making them a snack).

As with all the exercises, you can record this script yourself, pausing at the ellipses (. . .) to give yourself time to feel the relaxation that happens; you can ask someone to read it to you; or you can listen to me guiding you through the experience by ordering the audio recordings at www.worrysolution.com.

Take a few moments now to get yourself in a comfortable position, either sitting, reclining, or lying down. Loosen any restrictive clothing or jewelry so that you can breathe deeply and easily. Make sure you're in a place where you won't be disturbed for about twenty-five minutes. Feel free to move anytime to get even more comfortable. If you find yourself falling asleep when you listen, you might want to sit more upright, or even keep your eyes half open, in order to better listen to the whole lesson.

If for any reason, you feel like stopping this process of relaxation, simply open your eyes, look around, and return your full attention to the outside world.

Before you start, scan through your body and mentally assess your stress and tension level on a scale of 0 to 10, where 0 is no tension at all and 10 is wired to the gills.

THREE KEYS TO CALMNESS MEDITATION

Begin by taking in a deep full breath...and then allow your exhalation to be a real "letting-go" kind of breath...letting your out-breath be a bit longer than the in-breath... Again, inhale, letting your abdomen expand, and filling the imaginary balloon in your belly...and as you exhale, let it be a real letting go as if you are letting go of any unnecessary tension or discomfort in your body.

Pause in your breathing at both the end of the inhalation and exhalation...just briefly...to notice the still point that is there...and let the out-breath be somewhat longer than the in-breath.........let yourself take six relaxing breaths according to whatever rhythm works best for you...and as you breathe this way, just begin imagining that you bring fresh energy in on every inhalation...and you let go of tension or discomfort with every exhalation...

After six relaxing breaths, let your breathing return to its normal rate and rhythm...and anytime you want to relax more deeply, let yourself take a few deeper relaxing breaths...

If anyone needs to get your attention for something important, they can address you directly and you can open your eyes, come fully alert, bring your complete attention to them, and respond if you need to.

Otherwise, just notice that sounds, voices, or things going on around you are really not important to your purpose right now...and so you can let them remain out in the background of your awareness...and continue to concentrate on the relaxation and comfort that is beginning to grow in your body as you let yourself move to an even deeper level of relaxation and comfort.

If you *do* get distracted at any time while relaxing, simply bring your attention back to wherever you are at the time and continue from that point. Don't try to catch up or worry about it. Just bring your attention back to whatever suggestions are being offered at the time.

Now let your breathing once again become natural and regular and easy, and let's begin to relax more deeply by simply closing your eyes and bringing your attention to your toes. Just notice what your toes feel like right now. Notice if there is any tension or discomfort in your toes and notice what happens if you invite your toes to relax and become more comfortable...simply invite your toes to be more comfortable...and notice what happens...Just invite your toes to relax...and notice how they respond...and allow your toes to continue to relax as you bring your attention to the rest of your feet. In the same way, invite and allow your feet to relax in their own way...releasing any tension that they don't need to hold...

Just invite and allow your feet to relax...and now your ankles... invite them to move to a more relaxed and comfortable state of being without any worry or any concern about whether or not they relax...or how deeply they relax...just notice what happens as you invite them to become more relaxed and comfortable.

Now become aware of the muscles of your shins and calves... all the muscles of your lower legs...and notice how they feel...and simply invite your shins and calves and lower legs to relax...notice what you sense or feel in your lower legs as they begin to relax in their own way...without worrying or struggling to relax...simply inviting and allowing your legs to move to a deeper and more comfortable state of being.

In the same way, notice now your knees...and invite your knees to soften and relax...notice the muscles of your upper legs, the thighs, and hamstrings, the front and back of your upper legs...inviting them to soften...to relax...and to release any tension they don't need to have...you don't even need to worry about what they need to have and what they don't need to have...just invite your knees and legs to continue to relax in their own way.

Now notice your hips and pelvis...inviting the hips and pelvis... the very bottom part of your back and your buttocks to soften and relax...releasing any tension your body doesn't need to hold in those areas...and allowing the whole lower half of your body to continue to relax in its own way...comfortably and easily...without effort or struggle...and letting it be a pleasant and enjoyable experience.

Now become aware of the midsection of your body...your waistline...your abdomen...your lower back...and your midback... invite that whole midsection of your body to soften and relax in its own way...move around gently until you find the best position for your back...the position where it feels most relaxed and at ease.... allow your spine to carry the weight of your back as the muscles on either side of your spine soften and relax...

Now notice your chest...and your rib cage...the muscles of the chest around, across, and in between your shoulder blades...and invite your whole chest and rib cage to soften and relax...to release any tension it doesn't need to have...to begin to soften and relax in its own way.

As you imagine the trunk of your body relaxing in its own way, let it be a comfortable, pleasant experience...again without worrying at all about how deeply you relax...or how you relax more deeply... simply inviting, allowing, and noticing any relaxation and comfort that you feel in your body...

When you are ready, bring your attention to your shoulders... and your neck muscles...and invite your neck and shoulders to release, to let go, and relax in their own way...softening...releasing... becoming more comfortable...feel the weight of your shoulders on your trunk as they let go, lower and become more deeply and completely relaxed, letting go of any unnecessary tension or tightness.

As your shoulders more deeply and fully relax, imagine a very pleasant sense of relaxation flowing down through your arms...and your elbows...so comfortable...down through the forearms...releasing and relaxing...inviting your wrists to relax...and your hands to be soft and at ease...all the way down to the tips of your fingers and thumbs, allowing the palms of the hands to become deeply and comfortably relaxed...let each of your fingers relax one by one... the little fingers...ring fingers...middle fingers...index fingers...and thumbs.

Take a moment to slowly and gently turn or stretch your neck, allowing any tension or tightness to soften and melt away...feel all the muscles in your neck and shoulders soften and relax as you gently stretch. Feel any pain or discomfort melt away, and all the tissues relax as they soften and become more comfortable. Find the position where your neck and shoulders feel most comfortable and at ease...and notice how much better that position feels...

Invite your scalp and forehead to soften, relax, and to become cool, soft, and at ease...feel any tension in your scalp or forehead melt away as they become softer, cooler, and more relaxed. Notice the muscles of your face...and jaw...and invite your face to be soft, cool, and at ease...releasing any tension your face doesn't need to hold...relaxing even more deeply...and comfortably.

Notice the little muscles around your eyes...and invite the little muscles all around your eyes to soften and relax...to release any pain, tension, or tightness they don't need to hold. Allow that pleasant feeling of relaxation to spread all through your face and jaw muscles.

As the muscles of your face, temples, and forehead become

more soft and at ease, invite the muscles of your jaw to relax even more deeply...as the muscles of your jaw and even your tongue relax, your upper and lower teeth may feel like drifting apart a little bit and that's perfectly all right...feel any tension or tightness in your jaw melt away, as it softens and becomes more relaxed.

You might even want to invite your tongue to soften...and puddle in your mouth...and to relax deeply...and be comfortable...

Continue to breathe easily, and if there's any part of you that is not yet deeply and comfortably relaxed, invite those parts to find their way to an even deeper state of relaxation... And when you're ready to go even deeper and become even more relaxed, imagine yourself going to a place of great beauty and safety and comfort to you...it may be a place you have been before, or a place that simply comes to mind right now...either is fine, just choose a place that is very beautiful to you, a place that is very safe, a place you feel good to be in, a place where you feel comfortable and at peace...

Imagine now that you're in this place you love to be...this place that feels so good to be in...and if more than one place comes to mind, simply pick the one that attracts you the most right now...and imagine that you are there now...and notice what you see...notice the colors and shapes...the things you see or imagine seeing here... and notice what you hear, any sounds you might imagine hearing in this place...or perhaps it is just very quiet and still...you may imagine a fragrance or aroma, or a way that the air smells or feels...

And whatever you notice is okay...just notice whatever you notice...notice what time of day it is, what the temperature is like, and what season of the year...and especially notice any feelings of comfort, peacefulness, or relaxation you feel in this place...

Notice where you feel most relaxed and comfortable and imagine getting comfortably settled there...fix this spot up any way you want, to make it even more comfortable...more soft or firm, more horizontal or vertical...just right for you. Now imagine sitting down ... or lying down ... or taking whatever position you imagine to be most comfortable for you. Stretch out gently, and notice how good it feels to really let go and relax ...

As you imagine yourself becoming even more comfortable and relaxed in this place, allow yourself to enjoy these feelings in your own way ... with nowhere else to go ... and nothing else to do ... simply allowing the feelings of relaxation to deepen ... and enjoying how comfortable it feels ... letting this place become even more and more comfortable to you ... as you become more and more comfortable in this place ...

You can continue to enjoy relaxing here for as long as you like ... in this quiet, peaceful, beautiful place ... with nowhere else to go ... and nothing else to do ... except to relax ... and enjoy yourself ...

And take as long as you like in this place ... and know that while you simply enjoy a few quiet minutes here, your body and mind are not only relaxing, but refreshing themselves, rebuilding, and becoming stronger ...

And when you are ready to return to the outer world, all you need to do is prepare your mind ... look around your special inner place once more ... and remember that this is a special place for you ... a place you can come to anytime in your own mind ... a place of deep comfort ... of great physical and mental healing ... and you can come here anytime simply by relaxing your body and recalling what you see, hear, smell, and especially feel in this place ... and, knowing that, when you decide to return your awareness to the outer world, you can continue to appreciate the sense of relaxation and comfort you have experienced here ... and feel good about learning new skills that relax your body and mind ...

Remind yourself that you can bring about this wonderful feeling of relaxation anytime you like, simply by repeating the steps that you have learned here, beginning with your breathing ... letting your out-breath be a real "letting go" kind of breath and then simply just noticing, in order, the different parts of your body and inviting them to relax and release any tension they don't need...and recall what you see, hear, and feel in your special place of peace...Now, to bring your attention back to the outer world, all you need to do is simply begin to notice what is going on in the outer world around you. Begin to notice what you hear in the environment around you. Begin to think about bringing your attention back to the outer world, as if you are waking up from a very refreshing, very relaxing nap and just gently bringing your attention back to the outer world around you...

And when your attention is all the way back to the outer world around you, all you have to do is to open your eyes and feel yourself return all the way into your body...wiggle and stretch your fingers and toes, and feel like you are coming awake from a very refreshing nap...bringing your attention all the way back to the outer world and looking around, noticing what you see and hear, coming all the way back, feeling more refreshed, more comfortable, more relaxed than before and ready to make the most of the rest of your day.

You may want to take a few minutes to check in again and scan your body with your awareness...on a scale of 0 to 10, where 0 is no tension and 10 is the most you can have, where do you put your tension level now? Is this the same, less, or more than before?

Take some time to write or draw about your experience...

REVIEWING YOUR THREE KEYS
RELAXATION EXPERIENCE

What did you notice as you experimented with this relaxation method?

What was easiest for you, and what, if anything, seemed harder?

Were there areas of your body that relaxed most easily? Any that had a harder time relaxing?

Where did you imagine yourself going? What did you notice there?

Did anything surprise you about this experience?

Did anything bother you, or do you have any questions about this way to relax?

How Often Should I Practice the Three Keys Relaxation?

When I see a patient with a stress or anxiety-related problem, I ask them to practice a relaxation method like this twice a day for three weeks in order to begin to create new brain pathways and make the feeling of relaxation as familiar as the feeling of tension they are used to living with. If you are habitually tense, I recommend that you do the same. Set aside a half hour twice a day to practice this and other "worrying well" skills, and notice what happens to your tension levels.

You'll find that sometimes you relax very quickly and very deeply and other times you may have more trouble. The more you practice, the more consistent your relaxation will become. Soon you will be much more in control of your worry and stress.

How Do Relaxation and Imagery Relate to Hypnosis, Meditation, and Other Mind/Body Approaches?

Since imagery is a natural language of the unconscious, a coding language intimately related to our feelings, experiences, memories, and visions, it is involved in nearly all mind/body approaches to wellness and healing.

Common mind/body methods include relaxation techniques, meditation, hypnosis biofeedback, and "body/mind" approaches such as yoga, tai chi, and qi gong. When you closely examine what actually happens in each of these practices, you find it almost always has to do with imagery—whether focusing on it or letting it go.

Relaxation techniques are the most widely used, easily learned, and generally useful mind/body techniques because stress is often a significant factor in illness and health-related issues. The easiest and most effective technique I have found for relaxation is the one that you have just learned—abdominal breathing, muscle relaxation, and imagining going to a peaceful, safe place to take a five-to-twenty-minute daydream vacation.

There are many forms of meditation, but the most common ones almost always involve concentrating your attention on either a neutral or meaningful focus—a single word, image, sound, external object, or one's breath. *Vipassana*, or mindfulness meditation, teaches you to simply observe whatever is happening at the time as a focus of meditation.

Meditation tends to create a physiologically relaxed state and helps develop peace of mind partly because it prevents your mind from being carried away by your fears. In essence, it is a way to free your mind from its attachment, fascination, and perhaps even addiction to fearful and worrisome thoughts. Meditation can often be a first step toward being able to use your imagination for your benefit. When you repetitively return your attention to your mantra, your breath, or whatever meditative focus you select, you are making a choice to let go of your worrying, at least for the time being. Almost every major religion teaches some form of meditation, but as Harvard professor Herbert Benson has shown, the stress-relieving benefits of meditation are universal in that they create a "relaxation response" in the body that is the opposite of the stress response.

As useful as meditation can be, it isn't the entire answer to solving life's problems, nor is it a complete answer to stress, anxiety, and worry. It is a peaceful but somewhat passive response to life's challenges. Turning off the stress temporarily doesn't help you resolve situations that need resolving. That's where active, purposeful mental techniques utilizing imagery and autosuggestion, like the Inner Wisdom, Positive Worry, Effective Action, and Best Quality guided imagery processes you will soon learn, can take you beyond simple relaxation and help you access your inner wisdom, shift your mood beyond neutral into positive, and build personal strengths that can help you cope with worry and stress. The guided imagery techniques you will learn are forms of active meditation that give you a focus of attention but can also lead you to insight, motivation, and changes that you desire. Guided imagery is a form of meditation that is easily acceptable to the Western mind because while it can be used for relaxation, it can also be used for active problem solving.

People beginning to work with guided imagery often have concerns or questions about its relation to hypnosis, a much misunderstood phenomenon. Guided imagery and hypnosis are different, although there is much overlap between the two. Hypnosis simply refers to a mental state of relaxation and focused attention. Hypnotic states occur naturally, whenever your attention is highly focused. Everyday hypnotic states often occur when you watch movies or television, get thoroughly immersed in a good book, work on the computer, or drive long distances. When you are surprised that you've just driven 150 miles, or that it's three o'clock in the morning when you only intended to read for half an hour before going to sleep, you have been in a hypnotic state, where time distortion is a common occurrence.

The tendency to go into a hypnotic state varies among individuals, although most people are capable of focusing in this way. Many people worry that hypnosis is a mystical interaction where the hypnotist "takes over" your mind and can make you do things you wouldn't normally do. This fear comes largely from stage and television hypnosis acts that appear to do just that. Stage hypnotists use a variety of techniques to be successful, beginning with selecting audience members who are primed and ready to do what they ask them to do. They watch the audience for people who are laughing at their jokes, nodding, or leaning toward them when they move or gesture. This identifies people who are already favorably disposed toward the hypnotist. Once such people are called onstage, the pressure to comply with suggestions mounts, amplified by the disorientation and anxiety most inexperienced people feel onstage. This results in these people being very likely to do what the hypnotist suggests, after going through whatever ritual they are told will put them into a "trance."

The truth is, they are already in a state where they are likely to accept suggestions, and they were before they were selected from the audience. Stage hypnosis is entertaining, but using hypnosis therapeutically or for self-improvement is quite different.

For our purposes, we are simply using our natural receptivity once we are relaxed and focused to concentrate on new ideas, images, and thoughts, in order to establish new thinking habits that relieve worry and stress and build calmness, confidence, and creativity. If you like the idea of self-hypnosis, call it that; if you don't, call it relaxation and imagery, or imagery-based meditation.

RELAXATION AND AWARENESS

All these practices are interrelated and they can all induce a state of deep, peaceful relaxation. Relaxing will decrease your background tension level, the first step toward eliminating unnecessary worry and stress.

When you relax, you can also become more open-minded, and when that happens, your mind is easier to change. When you are better able to choose your thoughts and images, you can be more powerful in cultivating positive effects in both your body and your mind.

Regular relaxation practice will decrease your baseline stress level and help make you less reactive to the stresses of the day, but it won't solve or eliminate all your worries. While you are practicing your ability to relax, please go on to the next chapter and begin to actively clarify, sort, and bring more wisdom to your worrying.

4. Clarifying Your Worries

＊

I have known a great many troubles,
but most of them never happened.

— MARK TWAIN

＊

The next step in the Worry Solution is to clarify your worries and sort them into two categories: those you can do something about and those you cannot. Sometimes this will be easy, but sometimes you may be stumped by some of your concerns and have some trouble knowing to which category they belong. This is why one of the requests made in the Serenity Prayer is for the "wisdom to know the difference." We all have much more wisdom inside us than we use. This is especially true when we are anxious, stressed, or worried, because fear tends to cause a psychological phenomenon called regression. When we regress, we become more childlike in our thinking and feeling. The fear stimulated by uncertainty and lack of control may remind us of earlier occasions when we felt the same way, and those memories trigger other fearful memories. Feeling like a frightened child, we may not have good access to the wisdom, courage, creativity, or power we've developed as adults.

Research shows that when we are in certain chemical (emotional) brain states, it is easier to access memories and feelings that we had when we were previously in that same state. It is also more difficult to access thoughts that are not connected to that emotional state. When we are angry or scared, it's easy to connect to other angry or scared thoughts and feelings, but harder to connect to those that may be calm or forgiving. This phenomenon is called state-dependency.

Donald Overton, a psychologist at Temple University, first demonstrated state-dependent learning in 1961 with laboratory rats running mazes. Overton trained a group of rats to run a maze, then gave them pentobarbital, a strong sedative. The drugged rats forgot how to run the maze and stumbled around banging into walls and making wrong turns like a drunk trying to walk home after a bender. When the drug wore off, they could once again run the maze properly.

The surprise came when Overton trained another group of rats to run the maze while they were already dosed with the drug. They got very good at running the maze while they were bombed. When Overton withheld the drugs, though, and the rats tried to run the maze sober, they made many errors and eventually had to relearn to run the maze as if it were brand-new to them. If he drugged them again, they could once again run the maze easily and correctly.

In other words, memories encoded in one chemical brain state may not be available when that chemical state changes. Since emotions are distinct chemical states in important areas of the brain, changes in your emotional state may well alter your ability to access particular information or abilities in your brain.

We see state-dependency in everyday life. Have you ever gotten mad at your spouse and all of a sudden you remember everything he or she ever did that made you angry? Emotional memories seem to be filed according to the emotions they create as much or more than they are by their content.

To best use your mental resources, you need to shift out of a frightened state to one that will open the emotional doors to a broader range of memory and experience. Becoming an observer of your own thoughts will help you do this relatively quickly.

Who, Actually, Is Worried?

To help you clarify and sort your worries more easily, it will help if you take a mental step back and learn to observe your thoughts. Most of us think that we *are* our thoughts, or our minds, and that makes them difficult to change.

I remember clearly when I first discovered that I was not my mind. Like most young doctors, I had always been praised and rewarded for being smart, and I deeply identified with my ability to think well. A few years after I graduated from medical school, I found myself in a psychosynthesis training. Psychosynthesis is an approach to psychology initially developed in the first part of the twentieth century by Roberto Assagioli, an Italian psychiatrist who was a contemporary of Sigmund Freud and Carl Jung. Assagioli felt that Freud's focus on the unconscious as a repository of repressed urges, drives, and experiences was too limited. He taught that the unconscious was also a rich source of insight, creativity, and inspiration. He pointed out that many of our finest and most desirable human qualities, such as generosity, inspiration, joy, and altruism might commonly be undiscovered, undeveloped, or repressed. Assagioli's model of the psyche posited an entity he called the "Self," which he described as a center of consciousness that acts through the body, the emotions, and the mind. It is akin to what many call the soul, or the Hindu concept of *atman* (one who watches). It is that fundamental aspect of ourselves that never changes, no matter how old we get or how many experiences we have.

The observing self (whether you use a capital *S* or not) is a hard thing to explain, so our training class was guided through a practical experience. We sat comfortably on the floor and tuned in to the sensations we felt in our bodies—the weight of our bodies, the movement of our breath, the different feelings where we were clothed and not clothed, any tension or pain we may have been feeling. Then the teacher asked, "Who is this that can observe the sensations from my body?" No answer was required; it was simply an invitation to be aware. It was clear to me that though I felt my body, I was also observing my body, and therefore I was more than just my body.

We did the same exercise with our emotions—noticing how we were feeling at the time and how we felt about various people and events in our lives. The question again came: "Who is this that can observe your feelings?" Again, no problem—it was simply "me," the same me I had always known, the smart guy everyone had always told me I was, observing my emotions.

Then we were invited to notice the thoughts in our minds, and just to watch them, big or small, important or trivial: the shopping list, wondering what this exercise was all about, thoughts about getting uncomfortable on the floor, and so on.

We were asked to just watch our thoughts float by without trying to stop them, evaluate them, judge them, or interact with them. Then our instructor asked, "Who is this that can observe your thoughts?" As I noticed that I was watching my thoughts, something changed in me. I realized that if I could observe my thoughts, that meant I wasn't my thoughts any more than I was my body or my feelings. I couldn't really describe the place of awareness from which I was observing my thoughts, except that it felt very familiar and felt as if it hadn't changed much, if at all, during my entire life.

What's important about this experience? It means that if we learn to observe our thoughts and feelings we develop an inner "platform" from which to work. If we think that we *are* our thoughts or our feelings, it's hard to change them. When we become aware of our thoughts and feelings, we can make choices about which ones we focus on, which ones we energize, which ones we keep, and which ones we let go of or minimize. It's important to know that we have thoughts, but we are not our thoughts, and we don't need to be victimized by our thoughts. This awareness is critical for breaking up our habitual thinking patterns and worries.

Here is a very simple first experiment to help you get a sense of your ability to observe your thoughts. You will need a one-minute timer or have someone who can time a one-minute interval for you.

OBSERVER EXERCISE #1

Get in a comfortable position and make sure you won't be interrupted for five minutes. Feel free to move or change positions at any time to be even more comfortable.

Take a deep breath and when you exhale, let it be a real "letting-go" kind of breath, imagining that you can release a bit of tension, discomfort, or distraction with every out-breath…as you breathe in, imagine that you are welcoming in a fresh dose of energy and inspiration, because you are. As you breathe like this, invite your body to soften and become more comfortable, releasing and relaxing any tension or discomfort it doesn't need to hold on to…and don't worry about whether you need or don't need any tension…simply let your body become more comfortable, relaxed, and spacious…and gently turn your attention to your inner world…letting any unimportant sounds from the outer world be in the background of your awareness…and as you tune inside, just start watching your thoughts come in and out of your mind…don't follow them out, or try to block them… just observe the various thoughts…and now, set your timer for one minute and just count the thoughts that come through your mind… whether they are big thoughts, little thoughts, important, or trivial, don't even try to assess or analyze them…Just count the number of thoughts that come to your mind in one minute…

When the timer goes off, write down how many thoughts you counted…

REVIEWING OBSERVER EXERCISE #1

How many thoughts did you notice in that single minute?

What was it like to just be able to count your thoughts, without following them?

Do you have a sense that you have some type of "viewing platform" from which you can observe your own thoughts, feelings, and bodily reactions?

The average number of thoughts in a quiet part of your day is about a dozen or so. If you multitask a lot, or need to make many decisions a day, you may have more than double that number. If you do this experiment several times, you are likely to have different numbers of thoughts per minute each time. If you do it during or just at the end of your workday, you will probably have more, and if you do it early in the morning, you may have fewer, although every individual has a different pattern. There is no right or wrong number to have. It's just an easy way to get a sense of your ability to observe, rather than follow your thoughts.

As you move through the exercises, you will find the idea of a "viewing platform," from which you observe what's happening in your mind and body, extremely helpful. It serves as a vantage point to help you become more aware of which thought patterns serve you well and which do not.

PREPARATION FOR OBSERVER EXERCISE #2

This exercise, similar to the one I described going through in my psychosynthesis training, will help you have a clearer experience of the impartial observer inside you.

Make sure you won't be interrupted for fifteen to twenty minutes, and get in a comfortable position. Feel free to move or change positions at any time to be even more comfortable. Read slowly through this exercise or have someone read it to you with appropriate pauses, or get my audio recording of the exercise from www.worrysolution.com.

OBSERVER EXERCISE #2

Take a deep breath and when you exhale, let it be a real "letting-go" kind of breath, imagining that you can release a bit of tension, discomfort, or distraction with every out-breath…as you breathe in, imagine that you are welcoming in a fresh dose of energy and inspiration, because you are…As you breathe like this, invite your body to soften and become more comfortable, releasing and relaxing any tension or discomfort it doesn't need to hold on to…and don't worry about whether you need or don't need any tension…simply let your body become more comfortable, relaxed, and spacious… and gently turn your attention to your inner world…letting any unimportant sounds from the outer world be in the background of your awareness…and as you tune inside, notice any sensations that you feel right now from your body…any physical sensations you notice…the weight of your body where it meets the surface upon which you sit or lie…notice where your body weight is supported… and how you feel its weight…if your body was stamped on an ink pad, what impression would it leave from contacting the surfaces that are supporting it now?….Notice where you can feel the weight of clothing or covers, and contrast that to the sensations you get from where your skin is exposed…notice any sensations of warmth or coolness…notice any areas of tension or discomfort, and notice any particular areas where you feel relaxed and comfortable…notice the movement of your body as you breathe normally…where does it move and where is it at rest…what other sensations do you feel right now from your body?… … …

Now, silently say this to yourself: "I have all these sensations in my body and they bring me many experiences…I have a body but I am not my body…who is this that notices these sensations from my body?"

Don't try to answer this; just let yourself notice whatever you notice as you consider who or what it is that notices the sensations from your body…

When you are ready, begin to notice any feelings or emotions you may be feeling…think about some situations in your life that provoke feelings from you and simply notice how each feeling feels to you…notice where you feel them in your body, and what they feel like…

Silently tell yourself, "I have feelings and emotions, and they tell me what is important to me…I have feelings and emotions but I am not my feelings and emotions"…Then ask yourself, "Who is this that can notice the feelings and emotions I have?" Again, don't try to answer this with words; just let yourself get a sense of who or where you observe your feelings from…

When you are ready, begin to simply watch the thoughts that go through your mind…don't try to evaluate or judge them… and don't try to follow them or hold on to them…watch them go through your mind like you'd watch seagulls at the beach…don't try to keep them away, and don't try to keep them from leaving…just observe the thoughts as they come and go…notice the variety of thoughts…big, little…important, silly…deep, shallow…notice that you have thoughts, but you are not your thoughts.

And when you are ready, ask yourself, "Who is this who can be aware of my thoughts?"…

Again, not trying to answer in words, but seeking the experience of the observer, just noticing that you can, indeed, observe your thoughts if you want…

Take all the time you need……

And when you are ready, gently bring your awareness back to the outer world…feeling your body and gently stretching…opening your eyes, looking around, and noticing where you are…and when you are all the way back to the outer world, you may want to write or draw about your experience…

Reviewing Observer Exercise #2

What was most interesting to you about this experience?

Were you able to observe your body sensations, feelings, and thoughts?

How would you describe the place from which you were able to observe them?

What are your thoughts about this ability to observe your thoughts and feelings?

Remember, there are discussion groups, tips, support materials, and places for asking questions and sharing experiences at www.worrysolution.com.

Put Your Worries in Writing

Being aware of your ability to observe gives you a perspective from which you can become aware of and possibly change patterns of thinking and feelings that are causing you unnecessary worry, anxiety, and stress. You can now start to clarify your worries by simply writing them all down.

Writing down your worries will make you more aware of the types and sources of your worries and help you begin to sort out and prioritize them. You'll need paper and pen, a computer, or some other way of writing.

Set an alarm for ten minutes. Once you start the timer, jot down everything that is worrying you, in no particular order. Just include everything that you worry about, whether big or small, important or petty, or whether you think it is worth worrying about or not. If you run out of worries before the ten minutes are up, think a little more and make sure you include everything. If nothing else comes up, that's just fine. If time runs out and you're still writing, that's okay, too; just use what's on your list for this exercise and then come back and repeat it as many times as needed to get everything on the list.

Managing Your Anxiety While You Write Down Your Worries

Writing down and thinking about all the things that worry you can itself be a bit anxiety-provoking, but it is a step toward having less worry, so stay with it. There's not going to be anything on your list that doesn't already worry you.

If you find yourself getting tense or anxious while you're writing, take a breath and scan your body. Where would you rank your tension level on an imaginary 0-to-10 scale, where 0 is no tension or anxiety and 10 is the most you can imagine? What level is tolerable to you?

Use the relaxation skills you have learned to lower your anxiety level enough so you can continue to explore or learn. Use your belly breathing, relax your muscles, and go to your peaceful place until you bring your anxiety down to a manageable level. (Most people find this to be at 3 to 4 or less on a scale of 10.)

Take as much time as you need to finish your list. There's no hurry. Take a break anytime you want to, then return to the exercise and stay with it until you are done, or until you need another relaxation break. Breaking for relaxation periods will give you good practice with your relaxation skills while you are dealing with difficult material. If you find you can relax while you are facing your worries, you are already better off than you were.

Sort Your Worries

Once you have your list (don't worry, you can add more if they come up as you go along), take a sheet of paper or a fresh window on the computer and divide it into three vertical columns. Mark the left column "Can Possibly Change," the middle one "Not Sure," and the right one "Cannot Change."

Can Possibly Change	Not Sure	Cannot Change

You've probably guessed what comes next. Go through the worries on your list and sort them into the proper columns. Put anything that is potentially changeable in the left-hand column, whether or not you intend to act on it, and whether or not it would be easy or difficult. Everything that you *could* change goes in that column.

Anything that you think you cannot change goes in the right-hand column. Don't count the possibility that you might be able to change a situation by imagining that it changes. We will discuss the action of visualization or focusing intention later, but for now, this column is for all the things that you cannot change with a physical or mental action—like the passage of time, the weather, the Chicago Cubs' chances of winning a World Series, or the fact that we are mortal.

Anything that you cannot decide to put in either the left or right column goes in the middle "not sure" column. When you are done sorting your worries, take another five minutes or so to take a closer look at this middle column. As you consider each of the worries listed there, think about whether you could possibly change some aspect of each situation, and if so, move that piece of the worry to the left-hand column. Any aspect that you cannot imagine changing, put in the right column. Any situations you remain unsure of leave in the middle column.

This simple process sometimes provides interesting insights. Rachelle, one of my Worry Solution class members, noticed that there were no items in her "cannot change" column, but she saw that she didn't have time to address her "can possibly change" list because she was so busy fixing everyone else's problems! Other class members were surprised at how many items fall into the "cannot change" category. For some of them, simply looking at the written list of things they could not do anything about stimulated a sense that they could let go of them, or worry about them less.

Once you've listed and sorted your worries, go down each column and place a number from zero to ten next to each to indicate how much distress each worry causes you. Ten denotes something agonizing that causes you tremendous distress, and 0 means it doesn't really bother you at all (and probably shouldn't even be on the list).

Here's an example of how this process worked with one class member. Arthur had a lot on his plate and sometimes felt like he was going to come unglued. A fifty-eight-year-old dentist, he'd had a satisfying professional life but had made some bad financial investments, so when the stock market crashed and his house lost 40 percent of its value, his retirement plans essentially disappeared.

Arthur was significantly overweight, his cholesterol and

blood pressure were high, and he had some early indications of heart disease. His thirty-two-year-old son had still not identified what he wanted to do in life and after five-plus years in college had worked at a variety of low-level jobs interspersed with long periods of unemployment. Arthur had been helping him financially and things were tense between them. His daughter, on the other hand, was an A student in college but had ambitions to be an artist, and he worried about her ability to make a living. Just before the crash he had felt fortunate to have qualified for college loans that now loomed as $80,000 in additional debt that he had to pay off.

Married for twenty-eight years, he loved his wife, but she constantly complained to him about money, though she resisted his suggestions about earning some herself. She continued to spend as she did before the crisis and showed no signs of slowing down or caring about his predicament.

Most worrisome of all was that his eighty-four-year-old mother was showing signs of dementia, and he and his siblings were starting to squabble about who would need to be responsible for her care if she got worse.

Arthur wrung his hands as he talked about his worries, and at times he was fighting back tears. He felt that he was struggling with depression, and he was not sleeping well, which made everything more difficult.

I asked Arthur to list all the things he was worried about, without bothering to rank them or judge them, and when he was done, his list looked like this:

1. Mother's health and care
2. Income vs. expenses
3. Ability to keep working (his own health)
4. Wife's spending

5. Son's ability to support himself
6. Daughter's future
7. Value of his house and investments

Then I asked him to go through the sorting exercise above and rank his concerns on a 0-to-10 scale. When he was done, his list looked like this:

Can Possibly Change	Not Sure	Cannot Change
Income/expenses 10	Ability to work 10	Mother's health 4
Mother's care 8	Wife's spending 6	Value of house 4
Value of investments 8	Son's ability to support self 6	
	Daughter's future 6	

Interestingly, Arthur had at first ranked the two worries in the "cannot change" column at a level of 8, but once he wrote them in the "cannot change" column he downgraded them to 4, saying, "Why bother worrying about them when I can't do anything about them?"

ARTHUR'S INNER WISDOM

Because there were so many important things in Arthur's "not sure" column, I invited him to take a journey inside and imagine he was connected to a wise, loving figure that represented his inner wisdom. An image came to mind of his father, who was now deceased but who had been a very loving and reliable source of guidance to Arthur when he was alive. Arthur was quite moved as he imagined being with his father again, and was surprised at how real it felt. With my prompting, he thanked the image for coming and asked it if it would help him figure out what to do about his worries.

As we reviewed the concerns on Arthur's list, the image of his father seemed to communicate that he understood how hard it was to bear these burdens. He had been frightened himself during the Great Depression but knew he had to stay strong because so many people depended on him. He told Arthur that this was what a man does for his family, and that he was proud of him.

Arthur's father image told him that it was important to move his "ability to work" into the column that he could do something about, and that the most important thing he could do was to begin taking care of himself physically, emotionally, and spiritually. Exercising, eating better, and getting some emotional support would help him sleep better, give him more energy, and support his ability to continue working. Feeling better, and embracing the challenge would help him avoid falling into helplessness and depression.

His father figure also told Arthur that he needed to lovingly but very clearly let his son know that he needed not only to take care of his own needs but also try to contribute something back to the family. He said that letting the son know how much his help was needed would give his son something meaningful to do and help bring out the best in him.

Arthur asked about his daughter, and his inner wisdom image said to fully support her emotionally in pursuing her artistic path while making it clear that she also needed to find a way to support herself while she did that.

This was getting to be a lengthy inner discussion, and Arthur had had enough for one day. His father figure agreed to come back at any time, and after Arthur thanked this source of wisdom and guidance, he brought his attention back to the outer world.

Afterward, Arthur still felt sad and stressed about all the difficulties that had befallen his family, but he no longer felt as helpless. He started a regular routine of exercise and cut his food portions back. He quit drinking wine with dinner and soon began sleeping better. His mood improved. As he felt better he also felt more confident and grateful for his ability to provide not only high-quality dental work for his patients but sustenance for his family. He found that regular relaxation and meditative time was also very good for him. In his meditations he often imagined being with his father, enjoying his company when things were going well and asking for guidance when he felt stuck with a problem.

The Inner Wisdom meditation can be tremendously useful when you can't figure out what to do with some of your worries. I will teach it to you in the next chapter, and you should start with that if your most important worries are in that category.

Now That I've Got My Worries Sorted Out and Ranked, What's Next?

Look over your list and decide what particular worry you want to work with first. If you have a concern that you can't stop thinking about, or one that is much more important than the others, you may need to address that one first. If there isn't an overriding worry, though, pick one in the 5-to-7 distress range to start with.

If the first worry you have selected to work with is in the "cannot change" column, go to Chapter Six to learn how to either let it go or transform it into a positive form of worry. If it is in the "can possibly change" column, go to Chapter Seven to learn how to resolve it through taking effective action. If your most important worry is in the "not sure" column, go to the next chapter, to explore it with the help of your Inner Wisdom.

5. Inner Wisdom

*Wisdom can be learned by three methods: reflection,
the noblest; imitation, the easiest; or experience,
the bitterest.*

—CONFUCIUS

Some worries are complex, with tangles of issues that make it difficult to know whether or not you can do anything about them. Others may present moral or ethical dilemmas. When it's not clear what to do with your worry, bringing more wisdom to the situation can help you sort it out. Wisdom not only helps you understand whether or not there is something to do about a situation but also can help you decide if taking action is a good idea.

Wisdom is most often an outgrowth of age and experience, but it would be impractical to suggest that you wait thirty years to get a wiser perspective on worries that confuse and distress you now. Instead, let me show you how to shift your thinking so that you can use whatever wisdom you already have inside.

The word *wisdom* comes from the same root as *vision* and has less to do with being smart than with seeing how things fit into a bigger picture. A larger perspective gives you more understanding of a situation, allowing you to make better decisions. Wisdom combines rational and emotional intelligence with moral and ethical considerations. It comes from a whole-brain (rather than clever-brain) perspective. In the last chapter I shared Arthur's experience with you, an excellent example of how a smart man can become overwhelmed by worries and how his own inner wisdom helped him begin to deal with them more effectively.

Think about people who seem wise to you, whether you know them personally or not. What other qualities do they seem to have? Are there any qualities that they have in common? Are they fast, witty thinkers, or are they more considered when they offer an opinion about something?

In my experience, wise people are often a bit less glib in offering guidance or advice than quick-witted types. Maybe it has to do with their ability to listen from a broader perspective, or perhaps they have a better idea of what is really important. Maybe it's just that they seem to take more time to think, and the spaces between their thoughts allow wisdom to come through. Some brain researchers think that one biological basis of wisdom in elders is not just the fact that they have more experience but also that with aging comes a pruning of brain cells that increases the ratio of emotionally important memories to other memories and facts. The brain doesn't store many long-term memories that are not emotionally important. So not only does the wise person have intelligence, but that intelligence is held within the context of a bigger—largely emotional and relational—picture. The wisdom perspective very much includes not only the individual trees but also the forest and the wider area in which the forest abides.

Wisdom is more likely to come from within when you make some room for it. We might say that wisdom tends to appear in the spaces between our thoughts, and making those spaces bigger by quieting and slowing the thinking mind allows more room for our wisdom to emerge. You can use the relaxation skills you have already learned to calm and slow down the frenetic activity in your brain as it struggles with worry. A medical instrument called an electroencephalograph can measure the rate of electrical firing in your brain. When you are actively solving problems, your brain would operate at a baseline rate between 24 and 42 cycles per second, with most of this activity generated in the brain's "thinking" parts. When you breathe deeply and shift into a relaxation/meditation mode, the brain slows to 10–12 cycles per second, and as it slows even further, information from its nonverbal parts appear as images, feelings, and intuitions. The slowed activity level of your thinking brain allows these quieter messages from your emotional/ intuitive brain to emerge. Imagining that a wise, loving guide is with you in this relaxed but aware state of mind creates a conduit through which your inner wisdom can flow.

Before you go inside to meet with your own inner wisdom figure, though, let's consider some other ways that we can connect with wisdom.

Words from the Wise

Have you ever noticed how easy it is to give good advice to others? You may even find that the less well you know the person, the easier it is. Partly that's because you are not overwhelmed or limited by your emotional reactions, as you might be with a close friend or family member—or with yourself. When you are not overly anxious about the situation, the emotional distance lets you more easily draw on whatever wisdom you possess in order to offer advice that's not only rational but thoughtful.

One way to bring more wisdom into evaluating or resolving a worry is by talking with people whom you consider wise. Depending on the nature of the worry, of course, you will want to select people who can keep your confidences when needed, and with whom you can be honest. Listen carefully to what they have to say, and consider their advice. Take some time to see whether it fits for you or not. Whether to act on their advice is ultimately your decision, but listening to their viewpoints and noticing your emotional and intuitive reactions may help you clarify what is true and right for you.

The WWJBDLYD Approach

If you don't have any wise people you feel you can go to, consider seeing a professional counselor. Before you invest in that, however, take some time to ponder what a genuinely wise person would do in your situation. I call this the "what would Jesus, Buddha, the Dalai Lama, or Yoda do?" approach. Pick someone you see as an exemplar of wisdom and compassion, whether real or fictional, living or not, and imagine what guidance that person might give you if you had a chance to talk with him or her.

When Hillary Clinton was First Lady of the United States, she revealed that sometimes, when she was perplexed by a difficult situation, she would think about what Eleanor Roosevelt might do, and it helped her make good decisions. Of course, Clinton drew criticism from the usual quarters, charging her with magical thinking or spiritualism. But in fact Clinton's imaginative projection was a highly effective problem-solving device—a very normal and intelligent thing to do.

Eleanor Roosevelt was a brilliant and widely revered First Lady with a strong moral compass and an unwavering commitment to the public good. For Clinton to think about what Roosevelt might do in a difficult situation could very likely shine new and valuable light on it. Thinking about role models of wisdom can open our minds to possibilities and solutions that we may not have otherwise considered. That's what role models are for, after all—to help us become stronger, wiser, and more effective than we already are.

Back to Your Own Inner Wisdom

While thinking of others who are wise can help us access a certain amount of wisdom, it is even more powerful to go inside and invite input from a deeper, quieter, wiser part of our own brain. After all, our brain has been with us through everything we have ever experienced, and its main job is to learn from these experiences. In addition to what has happened to us directly, we've also observed others solving problems, read books, watched movies and television, perused magazines and newspapers, and followed current events to gain a tremendous wealth of knowledge. We have also inherited brain patterns that have evolved over millions of years of human life. Periodically slowing down our ordinary thinking brains through relaxation and imagery can let us draw from a huge interior reservoir of intuitive wisdom that can help us in unexpected ways.

Madeline, a twenty-eight-year-old secretary, came to see me

with a severe migraine headache. We had worked together before, so I guided her through a simple progressive relaxation
technique, asked her to focus directly on her pain, and urged
her to invite a wise, friendly image into her mind that could tell
her something useful about the pain.

She pictured a large mynah bird sitting on her head and
pecking away in the area of her pain. "Why is he doing that?"
she asked, and I suggested that she ask him, and imagine
he could answer in a way she could understand. To her surprise, the bird answered, "Why not? You let everyone else pick
on you!"

Madeline started crying and told me that the day before,
she had accidentally overheard a fellow employee making fun
of her in the coffee room. She started to get angry, but then got
nauseous, and started to feel a migraine aura. She went home
for the day and the migraine developed to the point that she
came to my office.

In her imagery dialogue, the bird agreed to work with her
to better understand and prevent her headaches. She left feeling 90 percent relieved with no other medical intervention.

Continuing internal dialogues with the mynah revealed
Madeline's long-standing pattern of low self-esteem and pas-
sivity. The mynah told her that holding anger inside led to her
headaches. I referred her to a good therapist, and after a while
she was much better able both to recognize her needs and
her feelings and to express them. Not only was she relieved of
headaches, but she was much happier and heading in a more
successful life direction. Her discomfort had led her to look
inside, and when she did, she found the wisdom she needed in
order to move forward with her life.

Listening to Your Own Inner Wisdom

So far you've learned how to use your imagination to help you relax by focusing on images that are beautiful and peaceful to you. Now it's time to learn to use the receptive power of your imagination to draw on your own deeper well of wisdom. You'll relax by going to your peaceful place inside, and then invite an image that represents your inner wisdom to come be with you there. Your inner wisdom figure (you can have more than one) can be an ambassador for your instincts, your intuition, and the relational wisdom that lives in the nonrational parts of your brain.

You may imagine this figure in any way—as a person, animal, spirit, religious figure, plant, presence, cartoon, movie character, or any other form that your imagination brings to mind. Don't try to decide in advance or anticipate what image your subconscious mind will conjure up. It may be a familiar figure or something completely unexpected. Don't get hung up about how it appears—for some people it is simply a feeling or a sense of being in touch with something wise and helpful. During the meditation we will carefully check to make sure it has the qualities we want most in a trusted guide—wisdom and a sense that it cares for you and is on your side.

First Frame the Question

Before you go inside to meet your inner wisdom figure, take some time to think about what you would ask if you were actually going to meet with a guide that was truly wise and compassionate. For our purposes here, pick one of the worries in your

"Not Sure" column to discuss with your Inner Wisdom. An obvious question would be whether you can do something about this worry or not. If it turns out that you *can* do something to change it, discuss with your Inner Wisdom figure what that might be. If it turns out to be something you can't change, ask for guidance in coming to terms with it.

You may find that once you are relaxed and engaged in the guided imagery conversation, your question will change. That's perfectly fine. Let this whole process be an exploration, with you observing as much as participating. Let the inner conversation unfold, and remember that you don't need to agree with the advice you receive. You are not committing to doing anything about the situation, just to considering it at a deeper, wiser level of awareness.

You will have plenty of opportunity to think about whatever information you receive and to make up your mind about what to do in the usual way. You are not going to lose your mind in this process—in fact, you're likely to expand it, and be better capable of dealing with whatever you have to deal with.

It will take a minimum of thirty minutes to get comfortable, do the guided imagery meditation, and have some time to write, draw, or reflect on what happened. Forty-five minutes to an hour is even better.

PREPARING TO MEET YOUR INNER WISDOM FIGURE

When you are ready, get comfortable, loosen any tight clothing, have something to write with nearby, and tell anyone who needs to know that you do not want to be disturbed for the next thirty to sixty minutes unless there is a fire or other true emergency.

Wondering how your inner wisdom figure may appear and what it may say, go ahead and explore this guided imagery meditation. As always, you can record this script for yourself and listen to it, or have someone read it to you, pausing wherever there are the three-dot ellipsis points (. . .) to let the imagery form or communicate with you. Just tune in and take however long you need, whenever you need it, and soon you'll find the right pace for you. To make it easier, I have professionally recorded this and all the other guided imagery processes in *The Worry Solution*. Ordering information is available in the Resources section or at www.worrysolution.com.

INNER WISDOM MEDITATION

When you are ready to begin, invite your body to move itself into a comfortable position, letting go of any unnecessary tension or tightness.

Start by taking in a comfortably deep, full breath, in through your nose and out through your mouth. Imagine you are breathing in feelings of relaxation with your in-breath, and breathing out any tension or discomfort with each breath you release...Take a few minutes to practice your belly-breathing rhythm, letting your exhalation be longer than your inhalation, and pausing at both the top and bottom of the breath...letting yourself release and relax with each breath...You may want to do that four to six times... just becoming more relaxed with each in-breath...and letting go of more tension with each breath you release...and anytime you'd like to relax more deeply, and concentrate more fully on your meditation, just come back to this special type of breathing, and let yourself relax and concentrate more deeply with each breath you take and release...

Now take a few moments to bring your attention to each part of your body, inviting it to relax and soften as we have before ...As you gently allow your eyes to close, bring your attention to your toes ... your feet ...and your ankles ...invite your feet and ankles to soften and relax in their own way ...allowing your feet and ankles to continue to relax ...bring your attention to your calves, and shins ...invite your lower legs to soften and relax in their own way ...releasing your knees and the large muscles of your upper legs ...your thighs and hamstrings ...just invite them to release any tension they don't need to have ...without worrying at all about how much tension they need to have and how much they can release ...simply continue to relax, allowing it to be a pleasant and comfortable experience, allowing your legs and feet to relax deeply and comfortably as every other part of your body relaxes more and more deeply.

Notice your hips, your pelvic area, and lower back, allowing the whole lower half of your body to soften and relax in its own way ... without worrying at all about how deeply relaxed you are or how you relax more deeply ...just allowing the feelings of the relaxation to move through your body without effort or struggle, and allowing it to be a really pleasant and comfortable experience.

Allow your abdomen to become soft and comfortable, and invite the organs in your abdomen to relax ...invite your lower back and waistline to relax as well ...notice your chest and rib cage and invite your chest and rib cage to relax more deeply and comfortably ... invite the organs in your chest to relax also ...and invite the muscles between your shoulder blades and across your shoulders to soften and relax as well.

And as each part of you relaxes, it becomes easier for every other part of you to relax and go deeper ...invite the feelings of relaxation to flow into your neck and shoulders, allowing your neck and shoulder muscles to relax in their own way, and imagine a very pleasant sense of relaxation flowing down through your arms, down through your elbows, your forearms, wrists, and hands ...all the way down to the tips of your fingers and thumbs, and the palms of your hands...deeply and comfortably relaxed.

As your body relaxes, allow your mind to become very quiet and still, yet very alert and aware...notice your scalp and forehead and invite your scalp and forehead to become soft and at ease...invite the little muscles around your eyes to relax, releasing any tension they don't need to hold right now...the muscles of your face feel soft and at ease...invite the muscles of your jaw to relax...and the muscles of your jaw and even your tongue can relax...your upper and lower teeth may feel like drifting apart and that's perfectly all right.

Continue to breathe easily, and if there are any parts of you that are not yet deeply and comfortably relaxed, invite those parts to find their way to an even deeper state of relaxation.

And when you're ready to go even deeper and become even more relaxed, and ready to learn something of great value to you about your anxiety...imagine yourself going to a place of great beauty and safety and comfort to you...it may be a place you have actually been before, or an ideal spot that simply comes to mind right now...either is fine, just choose a place that is very beautiful to you, and very safe, a place you feel good to be in, where you feel comfortable and at peace.

Imagine now that you are in this place of beauty and safety. If more than one place comes to mind, simply pick the one that attracts you the most and imagine you are there right now...notice what you see around you...the colors...the shapes...and the things you imagine seeing today in this beautiful, quiet, and peaceful place.

Notice whether there are any sounds you can imagine hearing, or whether it's very quiet and still...perhaps you notice an aroma, or fragrance, or a special quality to the air...and it's okay if you do or don't...just notice whatever you notice...what time of day it seems to be...what the weather is like...Can you tell what season it is?... Any season is fine.

Notice especially how you feel in this special place...notice any feelings of comfort, peacefulness, or relaxation that you feel and allow yourself to enjoy these feelings in your own way...with nowhere else to go, and nothing else to do, simply allow the feelings of relaxation to deepen and allow yourself to enjoy how comfortable it feels, letting this place become more and more comfortable to you...as you become more and more comfortable in this place.

And when you're ready, invite an image to appear of your inner wisdom, a figure that is very wise and very kind...simply invite an image to come and accept the image that comes into your mind, whether it is what you expected or not...and whether or not you think it's the right figure or not...Just let yourself receive for now the image that your inner mind brings to your attention...it may be a figure new to you, or a familiar figure, and either is fine...as long as the figure is caring, friendly, and wise...it may come in just about any form, as a person, an animal, a religious figure, a tree, a cartoon character, or anything else...simply allow it to be what it is for now and take a few moments to carefully observe how it appears to you...

As you observe the image of your inner wisdom, take some time to notice if you feel comfortable with it, and whether the image seems kind, caring, or friendly...

If, for any reason, the figure does not seem friendly or helpful, or if you don't feel comfortable with it, then send the figure away and imagine instead that you are there with an image that is friendly, helpful, and very wise...

In your mind, thank the image for coming and invite it to be comfortable there with you...allow it to respond and get comfortable... and when you are comfortable there together, imagine that you ask it its name...and imagine that it tells you its name...just accept the name the same way you would from anyone else...imagine that you can easily communicate with this figure and imagine that it can communicate with you in a way you can easily understand...

The figure may speak directly to you, or you may just know directly what it wants you to know…

When you're ready, ask it the specific questions you have about your worry or worries…and then pay careful attention to its response…it may speak to you, communicate directly or telepathically, or it may show you something in response…just allow yourself to be receptive to what it has to communicate for now…

Once you've heard what your inner wisdom wants you to know, take some time to consider what you've heard or understood… receive this guidance as if it came from a wise, respected teacher or mentor that you trust…

If anything is not clear to you, go ahead and ask any questions you have of your inner wisdom figure, and allow it to respond to each question…continue the discussion until you feel that you have learned all you can at this time…simply ask the questions you have and listen carefully to the responses that come back…

When you feel you've understood the guidance that's come today, take a few minutes to notice whether it has helped clarify whether or not you can do anything about the worry that you are wondering about…or whether you have learned anything that might help you resolve it…

If your wisdom figure has indicated an action to take toward resolving this worry, take a few minutes now and imagine how it would be if you acted on that advice…imagine how it would be if you applied this advice to your current situation.

As you imagine what it would be like to act on this advice or guidance, notice if any problems or obstacles seem to come up that might get in the way…and if such issues do come up, imagine how you might deal with them in a healthy and constructive way.

If you need some additional help with any of these issues or barriers, ask your inner wisdom how to deal with these obstacles or barriers…remember that this figure is here to help you find creative and wise options for addressing and reducing the sources of worry in your life.

You can continue to meet with your inner wisdom at any time by simply returning to your safe inner place and inviting your inner wisdom to come into your awareness, so you can discuss the issues and questions you have, and allow it to respond...listen carefully to what it has to share with you about these issues.

Of course, when you bring this advice back to your outer life, you will consider it again carefully and make whatever decisions are right for you...you will decide whether or not to act on any of this advice, or to come back and continue the conversation, until you find the solutions that work best for you.

Before you bring this conversation to an end for today...see if there's anything else you'd like to ask your inner wisdom and if so, do it now...and let it respond.

Take a few moments to silently review what's happened in this meeting...Notice whether you have learned anything about the issue you have focused on today...and pay special attention to anything that you want to make sure to remember or bring back with you when you return your attention to the outer world...

And before you return your attention to the outer world, be sure to thank your inner wisdom figure for coming to be with you today...and for being willing to help with your concerns...and if you haven't reached full clarity on the issue you've discussed today, ask it if it will think about it more for a while and meet with you again at another time...you may want to arrange a mutually agreeable time for a next meeting...

Then take your farewell for now from your inner wisdom, in whatever way seems appropriate to you...and allow the images to fade...and then as you appreciate once more the beautiful quiet peaceful place within you...recall just once more what you want to make sure to remember when you return fully to the outer world...

And then allow all the images to go back to where they came

from, and as you gently allow your attention to come back to the outer world, bring back with you whatever you've learned that seems important or interesting, anything that you want to be sure to remember.

And as your attention returns to the outside world, return completely and fully to your body, stretching, gently and smiling, and bringing back with you what is most important to remember...

Allow your eyes to open and look around the room, and come all the way back into the present time, coming alert and awake and refreshed and all the way back into your outer world...and take some time to write or draw about your experience, about what you've learned, and about any further questions that come to mind.

Remember you can come back to this special place and consult with your inner wisdom anytime you want to explore this or any other difficult issues that worry you...

Take some time now to record what happened in this meeting with your inner wisdom figure.

Reviewing Your Inner Wisdom Meditation

Take some time to write and/or draw about your meditation experience. Afterward, consider the following questions to help you better understand the nature of the advice or wisdom that you may have encountered.

What seemed most significant or interesting to you?

What image came for your inner wisdom figure?

Did it seem wise? How could you tell?

Was it kind and loving? Did you feel comfortable and safe in its presence?

What did you ask it?

How did it respond to your question?

How did you respond in turn?

What seemed most important or significant to you about this experience?

What are you bringing back from this experience?

Do you feel it clarified for you what you likely can and cannot do about this worrisome situation?

Do you have other questions you'd like to discuss with your inner wisdom the next time you meet?

Do you have other comments or questions about this experience?

Is There an Action to Take Now?

If you've found that the worry you focused on in this meditation is a situation you can do something about, move it to the left-hand column in your list; if not, move it to the right-hand column. If you still are not sure, repeat this process at another time and continue to discuss it with your inner wisdom figure until you have either reached a conclusion or decided that you can't act on it now. Wait a few days before going back to have another discussion with your inner wisdom about the same problem. During this time, your unconscious mind will be working on the issue and you may get more information in a variety of ways. You could have a dream about it, or you might become aware of something you hadn't noticed before. During this time synchronistic events may happen; someone may mention something applicable to your issue, or you may see a movie, TV show, or magazine article that is relevant. Just be aware that your unconscious mind is working on your question, so that you'll be sure to recognize helpful information when it appears.

After a few days, if this particular worry is still problematic, go back and discuss it further with your inner wisdom and continue to do so as long as you find it useful.

Once you have resolved or clarified this particular worry as much as possible, then choose another worry from your middle column for your next meeting with your inner wisdom. If there are more important worries in your other two columns, you can also consult with your inner wisdom figure about them.

As you work through each of these processes for separating, acting on, or coming to terms with each worry, you will find the process increasingly easier and more natural. Take the time to slow down, relax, and connect with your inner wisdom figure anytime you like in order to help sort out your thoughts and feelings about any situations that concern, distress, or perplex you.

6. Transforming Bad Worry

＊

*You've got to accentuate the positive, eliminate the
negative, and latch on to the affirmative . . .*
—JOHNNY MERCER, "ACCENTUATE THE POSITIVE"

＊

I think of "bad" worry as fretting about things you can't do
anything about and focusing on the outcomes that you don't
want to have happen. This is the worst possible way to worry,
because not only doesn't it solve the problem, it fritters away
energy and, worse, can frighten and depress you. By dwelling
on the terrible outcomes you imagine and turning them over
and over in your mind, you are in effect rehearsing failure. I
want to teach you some ways to either let go of or transform
bad worry into a much better way of thinking.

Elizabeth was an attractive forty-nine-year-old woman in a
good marriage with two healthy grown children, both successfully making their way in the world. She lived in a lovely house

in a safe neighborhood, and thanks to her husband's financial success, she was able to spend her days gardening (her passion), lunching with friends, volunteering at her community center, exercising, and visiting with her grandchildren and her mother, who was aging but doing it well. Elizabeth's health was good, but she found herself worrying more and more as she grew older. "I know it's silly to worry about most of the things I worry about, but I can't seem to help it," she complained to me. "I worry about my grandchildren, my mother, my children, the environment, the economy, the future, and the problems of people halfway around the world. I can't shut my brain off at night and am having trouble sleeping. What's going on?"

Elizabeth underwent a thorough physical exam and laboratory screening with her primary doctor, who pronounced her "healthy but anxious" and suggested she get counseling or consider taking antidepressants. A health-conscious person, she didn't like the idea of medications as a first resort and decided to consult with me instead. I ran some nutritional tests and also measured her hormone levels. These tests are important for women of her age, whose anxiety and worry levels may go up suddenly because of lowered or fluctuating estrogen levels in perimenopause, the years leading up to the end of menstrual cycles. Decreased or fluctuating levels of estrogen can cause insomnia, difficulty focusing, and memory loss, all of which tend to undermine a woman's well-being and self-confidence and to magnify the tendency to worry and become anxious.

Elizabeth's hormone levels turned out to be normal, so we talked instead about worrying and I led her through the clarification exercise in the last chapter. While she found that she could do something about a few of her worries (she decided, for instance, to sponsor several African children through her church program, and to recruit fellow parishioners to do the same), she concluded that much of what bothered her was beyond her control and she needed to learn to let go of those concerns or change the way she thought about them.

LETTING GO

I invited Elizabeth to create a ritual that would symbolize her choice to let go of the worries she couldn't do anything about. A ritual is a series of steps that represents a chosen action in symbols. There are rituals from every religious and spiritual tradition, or you can create your own. Rituals can be external, involving physical actions that may be witnessed by others, or internal, performed in the quiet and privacy of your own mind.

A letting-go ritual can be as simple as imagining a worry being held in your closed fist and then opening your fist to let it go. You can add words like "I now release my worry about XYZ," or you can simply say, "Good riddance." You can make your ritual more powerful by using mental imagery. You can, for instance, imagine that you feed your worries to hungry birds that gobble them up and fly away, or that you tie them to big colored helium balloons and let them go, watching them float away until you can't tell whether you can see them or not.

It's important for some people to physically carry out their letting-go ritual by writing down the worry and finding a way to release it. One woman wrote her worries on long blades of grass and released them into a stream, watching them float away until she couldn't see them anymore. You can also write your worries on paper and then burn the paper in a safe place and watch the worries go up in smoke. Your ritual can be as simple or as elaborate as you like. I suggest that the bigger the worry and the harder it is to let go, the more elaborate you make the ritual.

If a particular worry has occupied your mind for a long time, it is clearly important to some part of you, so give it the respect it is due and take time to feel the letting-go process. Whether you perform an external ritual or an internal ritual like the Positive Worry imagery you will learn later in this chapter, you may be surprised to feel both relief and perhaps some grief as you imagine letting go of a familiar worry. I believe this grief is related to the fact that even though you are accepting that you cannot do anything about this situation, you undoubtedly still wish that you could. It's appropriate to feel sad about letting go of something important, just as it's appropriate to let go of worries that you cannot do anything else about.

You will see that part of the power of Positive Worry imagery is that it doesn't require you to let go of your wish to see a situation turn out well. In fact, it encourages you to focus your mental energy on the outcome you desire. This practice relieves some of the anguish of feeling powerless, while you continue to wish, hope, and pray for a positive outcome. In essence, it gives you something to do about something that you cannot do anything about. The difference it makes in the way you feel can be like night and day.

The Illusionary Rewards of Bad Worry

I said earlier that worry is a natural function of the human mind and that it has an adaptive function when it allows us to solve difficult problems. But we also know that worry can easily turn from a tool into a tyrant, becoming a bad mental habit or even an addiction. That's because there are psychological, brain-based rewards for worrying, even when we worry about things we can't change.

The first psychological reward of worry is that it gives us an illusion of control. Worrying about something can partially satisfy a sense that we are controlling or doing something about whatever is worrying us. There's a well-known story about an old woman who would walk around her house three times every day, carrying a bundle of twigs and muttering to herself. One day a new neighbor asked what she was doing, and she replied, "I'm keeping my house safe from tigers." The neighbor said, "But we're in Indiana. There are no tigers here," to which the crone replied, "See, it works!"

The old woman was comforted by the magical-thinking function of worry. Worrying gives us a sense that we are doing something about a situation even when we cannot take direct action. That's not a bad thing as long as you worry skillfully, and as long as your "remedy" doesn't take over your whole life.

When the things we worry about do not come to pass (and most of the time they don't) we may feel safe and even powerful. The brain may interpret the connection between the worrying and the fact that the event never materialized as evidence that we are exerting some control over the situation. It's easy to see how this kind of "successful" worry can lead to an irrational yet powerful feeling that we can fend off undesirable events. This unconscious perception may well encourage us to worry even more.

The trouble is that this kind of worry is almost always distressing and uncomfortable, and sometimes it can even become obsessive, taking on a life of its own. Even more troublesome is that when we worry this way, our worries can act as autosuggestions. They can become significant, even dominant portions of our mental focus throughout the day, taking up more and more mental attention and energy, and creating the sense that life is even more frightening than it really is.

Research shows that when people are shown scary pictures, their anxiety levels increase. If you constantly think about scary images or terrible outcomes, it isn't surprising that your anxiety levels soar. Letting your imagination run wild can almost literally scare you out of your wits—which is unfortunate because when you are facing truly stressful challenges it is more important than ever to keep all your wits about you.

The Protective Function of "Bad" Worry

A second psychological function of worry is that it can "protect" us by distracting us from thoughts and feelings that might distress us even more than whatever we're worrying about. While this may postpone emotional pain, it prevents us from coming to terms with what's bothering us and keeps us stuck in a state of emotional limbo.

Nancy, a thirty-four-year-old graphic designer from South Carolina, had come to San Francisco seeking the creativity and tolerance that characterize this unique American city. She described herself as always having been anxious, as far back as she could remember. She had survived a difficult childhood, with an alcoholic father who was volatile when he drank. He could go from sweet and soft-spoken to yelling, angry, and verbally vicious with her entire family in the time it took to drink a few beers and maybe a shot or two of bourbon. While she didn't recall his ever raising a hand to her or her siblings, they constantly feared that his rage would spiral out of control and something bad would happen to them or their mother.

Nancy had consulted a therapist and found it very helpful.

Therapy helped her find the courage to leave home and come to California, and to start her own successful graphic design studio. Part of that success derived from her artistic talent, but even more came from paying attention to details and anticipating the needs of her clients. In this way, her tendency to worry served her well, because she rarely missed a beat in her customer service and job fulfillment.

Her problem, she told me, was that she "could never turn her mind off," and she felt stressed and exhausted all the time. She had taken several meditation classes but found that when she began to relax she got even more anxious and had to open her eyes and stop. She had tried several different methods, including biofeedback, where specialized equipment showed her how her body responded to her thoughts; the biofeedback therapist noticed that when she closed her eyes, the monitors showed that her body quickly moved into a stressful state of alarm.

Nancy told me that when she started to relax she felt an upwelling of strong emotion that was intolerable for her. Sometimes these feelings were accompanied by violent images of war or lurking predators, while at other times there was a panicky feeling without images.

Nancy was one of the approximately 15 percent of people who suffer from a condition called relaxation-induced anxiety. When they begin to relax in any way, often even when they simply close their eyes, their anxiety level goes up, not down. People with this condition have frequently suffered trauma as children, and as a result learned to stay highly vigilant about their surroundings. Research shows that the brain actually changes in children who have been abused or frequently frightened. The brain areas responsible for recognizing signs of danger or threat grow larger and these survivors become keen observers, ultrasensitive to signs of possible aggression or danger. They are often exceptionally intuitive, their senses are very keen, and their brains are working overtime to monitor subtle signals in the environment.

Research at the University of Pennsylvania has confirmed that worrying sometimes serves to protect people, whether or not they have been through trauma, from experiencing emotion-laden imagery or memories. The repetitive focus on the constant concerns occupies their minds so that more both-ersome, emotional, and difficult-to-process feelings are kept at bay. In this way, worry can serve an emotionally protective func-tion, but you will see that Positive Worry imagery can not only replace but also improve this function.

Worry Can Keep Us Connected . . . Sort Of

Worrying can sometimes serve as a marker of loyalty to the ones we love. Thinking about someone frequently is a sign that we care. But thinking of someone, sending him cards or emails, wishing him well, and worrying about him are not psychologi-cal equivalents. First of all, constantly worrying about someone, especially if you let him know that you are worrying about him, tends to diminish the person. When a mother worries about her children, even when they are grown, it's touching and nor-mal to some degree. But if you are forty-five years old and your mother tells you to make sure to dress warmly because it's cold outside, or greets you with a worried face and asks if you are feeling all right whenever you see her, it can have the opposite effect. Instead of conveying the message that she is interested in and wants to know all about you, it implies that you may be so incompetent and infantile that you don't know how to dress appropriately for the weather. The unbalanced focus on what is wrong, may be wrong, or could go wrong in the future overshadows the love and concern and drains the joy out of a conversation. It can become a communication barrier and create a wedge in an otherwise loving relationship. Mom (like all of us) needs to become more aware of what and how she is communicating if she is to have the best relationship with you. She needs to develop her skills and realize that her communications have multiple levels of meaning.

Interestingly, the same opportunities to either encourage or discourage competent behaviors crop up when we communicate within ourselves. This is essentially what the Worry Solution is about. It's about how we mentally process our world, what we say and imagine within ourselves, and how we can do that in a way that nurtures confidence and hope instead of fear, creativity instead of helplessness, and effectiveness instead of anxiety.

THE BIG DISADVANTAGES OF BAD WORRY

There are a number of problems with habitual, futile, "bad" worry. The first is that in spite of serving the psychological functions discussed above, it both creates and amplifies anxiety and stress in already stressful situations. Research at the NIMH Center for the Study of Emotion and Attention at the University of Florida shows that when people are repeatedly exposed to pictures that they experience as unpleasant, their anxiety levels increase; other studies reveal that when their anxiety levels are raised, people tend to look for and be more responsive to potential dangers, threats, and worries. The researchers used actual pictures, but it is reasonable to assume that reviewing your own internalized images and thoughts about unwanted outcomes would set off this same vicious cycle. In other words, your focus on the undesirable outcome is telling your unconscious mind to prepare for this eventuality. Even though many of these worries never actually materialize, the worry itself triggers anxiety and stress responses in the body.

Happily, other research, notably from Stanford University, has shown that anxiety-provoking stimuli and thoughts have two pathways through the brain. One is a primitive survival pathway, a direct "rapid transit" route from the emotional brain to the body that is triggered when we sense danger. This is a reflex response that happens in a fraction of a second, before we even realize what set it off. We hear a car backfire and we duck before we know whether or not it is a gunshot. At the same time a second neural pathway sends information to the thinking brain that further processes the relevant information, and we realize that there is no gunman. Recognizing that there is no continuing danger, the cortex sends all-clear signals down through the lower brain centers that turn off the fight-or-flight response.

Have you ever been surprised by a friend jumping out at you when you didn't know she was there? You have an instant fright response, but then if you see that it's a joke, the fear goes away very quickly. Whether you process it as a friendly game or a stupid unwelcome stunt determines whether you laugh with or become upset with your friend.

The point of this is that even if our first responses are reflexive and rapid, our thinking brain can modify the responses that come next. We get the opportunity to "re-respond" to the initial stimulus. In Chapter Eight I will introduce you to the important work of Dr. Jeffrey Schwartz, who has shown that over a short period of time people can actually form new nerve path-ways that can replace or modify the activity of well-established worry tracks in your brain by responding in new ways.

How Can We Change the Way We Worry?

Positive Worry imagery is a process in which you turn around your futile worries by imagining the best possible outcome instead of the worst. In this way, you are (1) still paying atten-tion to the problem at hand, so you are not ignoring it; (2) still occupying your mind with imagery, so your mind is not empty and open to uninvited thoughts and feelings; and (3) still thinking about the people, organization, or community that you are worried about, so it's not as if you are forgetting about them. The difference is that instead of focusing on the nega-tive imagery of the outcome you don't want, you are focusing on the outcome you do want.

You don't lose any of the potential psychological benefits of worry, but you shift your attention from negative, frightening imagery to imagery that is more hopeful, more positive, and just as realistic. After all, your hopes and fears are both prod-ucts of your imagination.

Positive Worry imagery often makes you feel that you have done something about a situation in which your options are limited or nonexistent, because, in fact, you *have* done some-thing. You have clarified, focused, and energized your inten-tion, desire, and will. You have symbolized and energized what would happen if you got to write the script, if you got to de-termine what would ultimately happen. To the extent that your thoughts can affect the situation, you have taken action, and if the outcome is not what you desired, it won't be because you haven't done everything you can. And it certainly won't be because you have been focusing your energy on the negative outcome.

How to Reduce or Eliminate Bad Worry

There are really only three things you can do with bad worry once you've identified it:

1. Accept that there is nothing you can do about it (or nothing you *will* do about it) and let it go.
2. Turn it into positive worry, focusing your intention, wishes, or prayers on the outcome you'd like to see.
3. Keep doing what you are doing.

Since you are reading this book, we can probably assume that doing nothing is not working for you, so let's look at how you can either let go of or modify your bad worry habit so that it is less distressing and may even become a positive force in your life.

Positive Worry Imagery

On the surface, Positive Worry imagery sounds simplistic and even inane, but it works—especially for worries that you either cannot or will not do anything about. I first learned this approach from my colleague Dr. Rachel Remen, who told me about using it with cancer patients that she counseled. I began using it with cancer patients who came to see me, and I was surprised how well it worked for them. After all, who is more worried than a person newly diagnosed with cancer? There is so much uncertainty in that situation, and people often feel helpless as well as terrified.

In Positive Worry imagery, you relax your body and mind and go to a safe, beautiful inner place, as you have before. Then you bring an image of the specific worry, one that you have decided that you cannot do anything about, to mind. You acknowledge that this is a real worry or fear, and also that it is simply that—a worry or fear. It is no more or less real than your hopes; it is simply a thought and feeling. You then choose not to put any more energy into this worrisome image or thought, and symbolize that choice in some way. I find that imagining a red circle with a slash through it stamping this thought out works well, but you may have a different image. The key is to create an image that symbolizes that you are rejecting this fear, and then shift your attention to an image of the outcome you would prefer. This shift of focus affirms your desire for a positive outcome and clarifies how things would turn out if you were in control. Then you let the worry go until or unless it comes up again.

Robert was a middle-aged physician just diagnosed with leukemia. He was extremely anxious about his diagnosis, his prognosis, and what he was facing in terms of treatment. He was trying to be positive about his situation but said he had been extremely frightened and anxious since hearing that he had cancer. I taught him Positive Worry imagery and he took to it beautifully. Every time he got anxious or noticed himself thinking about dying from his disease, he took a deep breath, mentally stamped out the worrisome thoughts or images, and visualized instead being at his son's high school graduation, which was about ten years away. He imagined himself in that happy future looking healthy, enjoying the company of his family, and feeling grateful that his treatment had been so successful. He said the process almost instantly calmed him down and gave him the feeling that he had some power and choice about what would happen to him. It only took him a few seconds to a minute each time, and the more anxious he was, the more he ended up doing Positive Worry. Robert and others in similar circumstances have thanked me many times over for teaching them this simple method.

If this guided imagery technique can be effective for worry and anxiety with the level of intensity that Robert felt, imagine how well it will work for you if your worries are not as frightening. If you practice the Positive Worry process every time an unbidden and unwelcome worry comes to mind, turning them into "positive worries" will quickly become a habit. Because you will be repetitively focusing your attention on energizing your hopes rather than your fears, you will at the very least feel better, and you may even be influencing the outcome as well.

Sheila was constantly worried that her fourteen-year-old son, Mark, wouldn't be able to handle the increased workload and social stress of high school. She worried about Mark's sensitivity and his small stature, and worried that he might be bullied or ignored by popular kids. Mark had, in fact, always done relatively well in school and had a small but close group of friends who would be attending the same high school. He shared with me that his mother's worrying not only annoyed him but also made him feel that there might be something wrong with him that he wasn't aware of. He himself wasn't worried about the things that bothered Sheila.

I taught Positive Worry imagery to Sheila, asking her to notice the negative thoughts she had about Mark's upcoming high school experience, and showing her how to convert them to positive imagery instead. I suggested that she try doing that for three weeks to see what happened. She began imagining him as smart, capable, and well-adjusted (which wasn't that hard, since he was all those things), and she shifted into Positive Worry whenever she began to fret about him. After a week or so she told me that she felt much more positive about him going to high school and was puzzled that she had ever become so worried about him. She felt more relaxed in general, especially around Mark, and he felt much more relaxed and comfortable with her.

Try the Positive Worry process and see how it works for you. I think you'll be pleasantly surprised. Pick a juicy worry from your "cannot change" column to focus on for this process.

Preparation for Positive Worry Imagery

The usual preparation for imagery work applies—take a comfortable position and make sure you won't be disturbed for twenty minutes or so. Read the exercise, or have it read to you, with pauses at the ellipses (. . .), or order the audio recording at www.worrysolution.com.

POSITIVE WORRY IMAGERY

Let yourself begin to relax in your own way…let your breathing get a little deeper and fuller…but still comfortable…with every breath in, notice that you bring in fresh air, fresh oxygen, fresh energy that fuels your body…and with every breath out, imagine that you can release a bit of tension…a bit of discomfort…a bit of worry…and

---

let that deeper breathing and the thoughts you have of fresh energy in and tension and worry out be an invitation to your body and mind to begin to relax...to begin to shift gears...and let it be an easy and natural movement...without having to force anything...without having to make anything happen right now...just letting it happen... just breathing and relaxing...breathing and energizing....

Come back to taking a few deeper breaths whenever you feel like relaxing even more deeply...but for now, let your breathing take its own natural rate and its own natural rhythm...and simply let the gentle movement of your body as it breathes allow you to relax naturally and comfortably...almost without having to try...

And noticing how your right foot feels right now...and how your left foot feels...and noticing that just before you probably weren't aware of your feet at all...but now that you turn your attention to them, you can notice them and how they feel...and notice what happens when you silently invite your feet to relax...and become soft and at ease...and also noticing how your legs feel and releasing your legs...and letting your legs respond in their own way...and noticing any release and relaxation that happens...without having to make any effort at all...just softening and releasing...and letting it be a comfortable and very pleasant experience...

And you can relax even more deeply and comfortably if you want to...by continuing to notice different parts of your body and inviting them to soften and relax...and noticing how they relax... and you are in control of your relaxation and only relax as deeply as is comfortable for you...and if you ever need to return your awareness to the outer world you can do that by opening your eyes and looking around and coming fully alert...and if you need to respond to anything there you can do that...and knowing that you can do this if you need to...you can relax again and return your attention to the inner world of your imagination...

Inviting your low back, pelvis, and hips to release and relax...and your abdomen and midsection ...and your chest and rib cage ...without effort or struggle ...just letting go but staying aware as you do ...

Inviting your back and spine to soften and release ...in your low back ...midback ...between and across your shoulder blades ...and across your neck and shoulders ...your arms ...and elbows ...and forearms ...through your wrists and hands ...and the palms of the hands ...the fingers ...and thumbs ...

Noticing your face and jaw and inviting them to relax ...to become soft and at ease ...and your scalp and forehead ...and your eyes ...even your tongue can be at ease ...

And as you relax, let your attention shift from your usual outer world to what we can call your inner world ...the world inside that only you can see, hear, smell, and feel ...the world where your memories, your dreams, your feelings, your plans all reside ...a world that you can learn to connect with ...that can help you in many ways on your journey ...

And imagine that you find inside a very special place ...a very beautiful place where you feel comfortable and relaxed, yet very aware ...this may be a place that you have actually visited at some time in your life ...in the outer world or even in this inner world ...or it may be a place that you've seen somewhere ...or it may be a brand-new place that you haven't visited before ...and none of that matters as long as it is a very beautiful place, a place that invites you and feels good to be in ...a place that feels safe and healing for you ...

And let yourself take some time to explore this place ...and notice what you imagine seeing there ...all the things you see ...and how you see them ...don't worry at all about how you imagine this place as long as it is beautiful to you and feels safe and healing ...and notice if there are any sounds you imagine hearing ...or if it is simply very quiet in your healing place ...notice if there is a fragrance or aroma that you imagine there or a special quality of the air ...there may or may not be, and it's perfectly all right however you imagine this place of healing...it may change over time as you explore it, or it may stay the same...it doesn't matter at this point...just let yourself explore a little more...

Can you tell what time of day it is...or what time of year it is... and what the temperature is like?...How you are dressed?...Take some time to find a place where you feel safe and let yourself get comfortable there...and just notice how it feels to imagine yourself there...and if your mind wanders from time to time, just take another deep breath or two and gently return your attention to this beautiful and healing place...just for now...without feeling the need to go anywhere else right now...or do anything else...just for now...

And as you relax in this special place of healing, let an image come to mind that can symbolize the outcome you would like to see from the worry you are aware of...simply allow an image to come that represents this to you—it may come in any form...it could be anything...how would you imagine the outcome you would desire if it were up to you?...Take your time and let yourself begin to imagine that outcome now....and don't worry at all about whether the image you have now is the best image or the strongest image... you may be aware of many images of your preferred outcome as you work through this process...and you may change your imagery many times to better fit your understanding of the process...but for now, let an image stabilize......and let this image be a symbol for the outcome you would have if you could write the script for this story... and imagine it happening now...and imagine it being as real as you possibly can...feel yourself energizing this image and consciously choosing it as your desire...if you need more power, imagine you can connect to people and things you love...and to whatever source of life and energy you imagine put you here in the first place...and imagine that those sources provide additional energy that you can invest in this image of desired outcome...

Take a few minutes now and imagine this happening in your own way and let whatever way you imagine this happening to be just fine for now....Your unconscious mind understands what your conscious mind is telling it...it understands that your intention is to activate and stimulate all the healing capabilities it has...and it knows just how to respond, however you imagine this healing...

Let this be your positive preferred image for now...let this particular image or "film clip" come to stand for the outcome you would have happen if you were in charge...and let a word or phrase come to mind that also represents this outcome...a word or phrase that both represents this choice within you...it may be something you've heard, or something that just comes to mind right now...Give yourself time to settle for now on a word or phrase that can remind you of your choice of focus.........

And anytime in the future that you find yourself worrying about this particular thing, let yourself consider whether it serves you to think about that...and if it does, let yourself think creatively about how you can resolve that concern......but as soon as you become aware that this fear or worry is simply a fear or worry, simply acknowledge it as that...and take a deep breath to begin to relax...and imagine that you cancel the fear or worry...you can imagine having a big red circle stamp with a slash through it and stamp that worry out...and become aware of the outcome you desire...and the word or phrase that reminds you of that...and let that symbol and imagery of your preferred outcome fill your awareness...and notice how it feels to choose and energize that preference...imagining it coming true...and knowing that the more you tune into this the easier it is to imagine and feel...

And you can let any good feelings that come with imagining this outcome grow stronger within you...and stay with you as long as you like...and even bring them back with you when you decide to return your attention to the outer world...knowing that choosing this focus is better than focusing on the other…and the more you choose where you put your attention the easier it can become in the future…

And taking all the time you need…And when you are ready to return your attention to the outer world, silently express any appreciation you might have for having a special place within you…and for being able to use your imagination in this way…and for the mental capabilities that have been built into you by nature.…and when you are ready, allow all the images to fade and go back within… and gently bring your attention back to the room around you and the current time and place…and bring back with you anything that seems important or interesting to bring back, including any feelings of comfort and relaxation…and when you are all the way back, gently stretch and open your eyes…and take some time to write or draw about your experience.

REVIEWING YOUR POSITIVE WORRY EXPERIENCE

Notice how you feel when you are finished with this imagery process.

What was this experience like for you?

Did anything that felt significant happen?

Do you feel different in any way? If so, how?

Do you sense any sense relief? Happiness? Sadness? Other feelings?

Do you have a sense that Positive Worry imagery can be helpful in changing the way you relate to worries that you cannot do anything about?

How might you remind yourself to repeat this process if this worry or fear comes up again?

You will probably find that your worries continue to pop back up, especially in the early days of this practice. If they do, just be patient with yourself as you continue to practice Positive Worry imagery for two to three weeks. The more you do it, the easier and more effective it will become.

Remember, you are building a new habit, and it requires a little time to take root and become second nature. As time goes on, notice how this process changes how often you worry, or how different it feels to worry in this new way.

You will find it useful to quickly use the Positive Worry process each time a worry resurfaces. You don't need to go through the long relaxation induction. Whenever a bad worry comes up, simply take a nice deep relaxing breath, let it out, acknowledge the worry, stamp it with the red circle and slash, release the negative thoughts from your mind, and focus instead on an image of the outcome you desire. Every time you do this, you reaffirm your choice to let go of your negative worry habit, and you put your mental energy into energizing a better outcome.

Remember Nancy, the young woman who had trouble closing her eyes because of the strong emotional images and feelings that came up? A variation of Positive Worry imagery was very helpful to her. I taught her to do this exercise with her eyes open without even trying to go into a deep relaxation. Nancy would just take a deep breath or two and the angry and violent images would come into her mind. She would quickly trap them in strong balloons and then imagine inflating the balloons with helium. She watched them float away and then blew them up with a powerful bazooka-like device. She had a great time watching them explode one after the other, and after a fairly short time they stopped coming as frequently. She was actually kind of disappointed when this happened!

Nancy would repeat this exercise once or twice a day or

whenever she felt anxious, irritable, or frustrated, and she found that within three to five minutes her mind would become pretty calm and peaceful. After a while I suggested that she could take a few minutes to go to a safe, protected place that was very beautiful to her if she wanted to prolong and deepen her sense of peacefulness. She took the bazooka with her for protection. This turned into a very effective meditation for her.

The psyche wants to move toward balance. In this case, Nancy's unconscious mind guided her to meet violence with strength and to symbolically be armed and ready to shoot down intrusive thoughts that distressed her. The experience of the strength and power that came with that big imagined weapon released some of the fear and anger that had previously plagued her, and instead provided her with some very welcome relaxation and a sense of safety. And nobody was hurt in the creation of this imagery!

Why Positive Worry Imagery Works

While this imagery process is quite simple, it works surprisingly well—better, in fact, than I thought it would when I first suggested it to my patients. After witnessing its effectiveness for many years, I believe there are some sound psychological reasons that explain why it works so well.

First, it begins with acknowledging the worry. It clarifies the issue and takes it out of the realm of vagueness, a quality that tends to amplify and prolong worry. It also directly deals with the phenomenon that results from trying *not* to think of the worry. Trying not to think about something always brings that thing to mind (try *not* to think about a rabbit for a minute), so the strategy is doomed to failure. Positive Worry takes the opposite approach: it begins with focusing on and symbolizing the worry.

Next, Positive Worry relieves you of trying to block the thoughts from coming and places the focus instead on your response to the thoughts. If you are a habitual worrier, the worrisome thoughts are just going to come on their own, and trying to block them out of your awareness is a waste of energy. Shifting the way you respond to them, however, is akin to the way a good martial artist sidesteps an attack and uses his opponent's energy to get the opponent in a position where he has little or no power. It is like a form of mental jujitsu.

Third, Positive Worry imagery lets you take action, even if it's a mental action. Your symbol of negation, the red circle with the slash through it (or whatever works for you), lets you mark the worry as something into which you choose *not* to put energy or attention. This ritual satisfies the mind's desire to do something about an untenable situation. You might even imagine a satisfying sound that goes with the stamping-out part of this process to make it more powerful.

Fourth, Positive Worry imagery requires that you imagine and symbolize the outcomes that you desire, giving you a clear focus of intention, choice, or prayer. Oddly, it gives you something to do about something that you have already decided you cannot do anything about!

Fifth, the shift of your attention from a flow of negatively charged images and thoughts to a mental slide show of positive outcomes is likely to improve your mood, even though you are dealing with the same issues.

Finally, repetitively shifting your attention to positive outcomes may actually result in growth in areas of your brain that start to do this automatically. My colleague Dr. David Bresler, a neuroscientist, always says that "what you pay attention to grows," and research proves him correct. Neuroscience journalist Sharon Begley wrote "Attention . . . seems like one of those ephemeral things that comes and goes in the mind but has no real physical presence. Yet attention can alter the layout of the brain as powerfully as a sculptor's knife can alter a slab of stone." She described an experiment at the University of California, San Francisco, in which scientists "rigged up a device that tapped monkeys' fingers 100 minutes a day every day. As this bizarre dance was playing on their fingers, the monkeys heard sounds through headphones. Some of the monkeys were taught: Ignore the sounds and pay attention to what you feel on your fingers . . . Other monkeys were taught: Pay attention to the sound."

After six weeks, the scientists compared the monkeys' brains and found that monkeys paying attention to the taps had expanded the somatosensory parts of their brains, where they would feel touch, but the monkeys paying attention to the sounds grew new connections in the parts of the brain that process sound instead. Researcher Michael Merzenich and a colleague wrote that through choosing where we place our attention, "we choose and sculpt how our ever-changing minds will work, we choose who we will be the next moment in a very real sense, and these choices are left embossed in physical form on our material selves."

Positive Worry imagery reduces worry, anxiety, and stress, which is what we are all about here. In addition to the psychological benefits and the potential brain rewiring, focusing on the outcomes that you desire may even alter the course of events in ways we don't really understand.

A Few Words About the "Secret"
of Mental Manifestation

A few years ago a book called *The Secret* was a big hit, garnering the attention of millions of readers and viewers. The "secret" that *The Secret* was promoting was that if you focus on your goals and desires, the law of attraction would make them magically come true.

I believe there is some truth to this, but I also believe that this so-called secret is really only half the secret to realizing your dreams. The other half (often much more than half) is actually doing what it takes to have your dreams come true.

One example they showed in *The Secret* was a man who had imagined himself living in his dream house, and now, to his astonishment, he was living in that exact same house. It skipped over, though, what he had to do to accomplish that—like make the money to afford the house, and have it designed and built! I was astounded that he was so astounded; he had worked for years to turn this dream into a reality.

It is true that your future often begins as a dream or vision, a creation in your imagination, and it is also true that the more you focus on any goal the more likely you are to reach it. When you throw the dart, release the arrow, or shoot the rifle it helps a lot if you concentrate on the target you want to hit.

Humans are built to set and reach goals. When we focus our intentions on a goal, all our inner resources begin to mobilize to make that happen. This ability is a good thing and we should use it. But I am not sure that it works primarily through a mystical or magical medium, though it sometimes seems that way. It may partially work by alerting us to people, things, and other resources that will help us reach the goal we have set. Have you ever noticed that when you buy a new car you then start seeing the exact same car everywhere? In a similar way, when you set a goal or focus your intention, your brain is vigilant for people, events, and other resources that will help you hit your bull's-eye.

Sometimes things do come to your aid that seem truly magical or not rationally explainable—meaningful coincidences (Carl Jung called them synchronistic events) that both help us along the way and expand our belief in the connectedness of all things. To me, synchronistic and fortuitous events are a bonus. They are delightful when they happen, but unfortunately, you can't always count on them.

In the movie *Little Big Man*, Dustin Hoffman plays a character who as a child is captured in an Indian raid on a wagon train. The chief, a wise and mysterious Native American elder, adopts him as a grandson. Late in the story, Hoffman visits this grandfather and finds that the old man is preparing for his death. "The time has come," the old man says as he lays out his power objects and begins chanting his death song. He spreads his blanket outside and after hours of chanting lies down on it to await his death. After failing to convince his grandfather not to go, Hoffman's character falls tearfully asleep. He awakens in the morning just as his grandfather is dragging his blanket back into the tepee. Looking at Hoffman, the wise old man shrugs and says, "Sometimes the magic works and sometimes it doesn't."

If the outcome you want spontaneously comes true as you focus on it, say thank you to whatever force or power you feel has responded to your mental focus and enjoy what has come through its grace. Consider it a gift and be grateful.

If you do not ultimately end up with the outcome you desire, at least you can know that you have done everything that is within your power to do. You have focused your energy on it; you have "voted" your desire. You haven't ignored your concern, but you haven't put any energy into the outcome you do *not* want to have happen, either.

OTHER THINGS YOU CAN DO TO REDUCE YOUR "BAD" WORRY HABIT

While most people find that Positive Worry imagery, whether they use it in the context of prayer or in a secular form, greatly reduces the amount and intensity of their worry, others will find that adding one or more physical rituals will help them even more. Here are a few outer-world approaches that also stimulate your inner mind to let go of at least some of your habitual worry.

Track the Outcomes of Your Worries

Take the worries you listed as ones you can't do anything about and keep track of them over time. See how many of them come true and how many of them don't. Tracking them over a period as brief as two to three weeks will give you interesting information about how often your worries come true. The longer you track them, the more you will learn about the nature of your worrying.

Research by psychologist Robert Leahy, Ph.D., of Weill Cornell Medical School and author of *The Worry Cure*, shows that 85 percent of worries don't have the bad outcome the worrier anticipates, and even when the worries do come true, 79 percent of people say they handled the outcome better than they thought they would.

Leahy recommends writing your worries down on a regular basis and noticing whether they come and go or stay relatively consistent. Many habitual worriers find that while they are always worried, the content is always shifting, which indicates that the worry is a habit, or serves one of the psychological functions I described, and is not really tied to external reality. This awareness in itself is a critical step toward being able to take control over your worry habit.

Delegate Your Worrying—Even to Nobody!

At the University of California, Davis, Medical Center's art therapy program for pediatric cancer patients, young patients with many genuine worries about their illness and treatment are introduced to worry dolls, little dolls dressed in traditional Guatemalan clothing that come in a tiny woven basket painted in bright colors. The worry dolls (sometimes called trouble dolls) are so tiny that half a dozen or more can sit in the palm of your hand. The children tell their worries to the little dolls before they go to sleep, then put the dolls under their pillows. The idea is that the dolls will worry for them while they sleep. Principal investigator Marlene von Friederichs-Fitzwater has found that this simple intervention helps the children sleep and reduces their worry level significantly. Interestingly, this method often works for adults as well, maybe because psychologically we are all children deep inside. Worry dolls are cheap, and you can even buy them from an organization that donates money to help feed and shelter the poor all over the world (log on to www.shop.thehungersite.com and search for "dolls").

Another traditional folk approach that works surprisingly well is to create a worry jar or worry box. Write down the worries you can't do anything about on little slips of paper and drop them in the designated jar or box before you go to sleep. That way you know they won't be forgotten, and you may be able to feel comfortable letting go of them for a little while.

While these methods may seem silly on the surface, they are based on rituals that go back to prehistory. They are related to prayer and magic, wishful thinking, confession, and surrender—all sound psychological principles that can be effective in helping us come to terms with things that are, essentially, unacceptable to and unsolvable by us.

Faith and Prayer

Our ancestors prayed to the unseen forces that they believed created their lives, asking for mercy, healing, and deliverance from pain, suffering, illness, loss, and death. While neither worry dolls nor worry jars are as sacred as prayer, the psychology behind their effectiveness is similar. First, the worry is acknowledged and named. Second, it is given up to someone or something that might magically take care of it. This is the essence of ritual, however simple or elaborate you choose to make it.

If you are religiously or spiritually devout, you may find prayer very helpful with bad worry. If you can pray with faith, request the outcome you desire, and release your worry into the hands of whatever higher power, deity, or force you believe in, you should gain some measure of comfort. If you are not a devout believer, though, the Positive Worry imagery will let you make good use of the same psychological principles.

The only difference between prayer and imagery is in whom you think you are addressing. If you believe in God or a higher power, then your prayer—asking for and suggesting a desired course of action—is directed to that power. If you don't believe in a deity, then you can imagine that your thoughts are directed to your own subconscious mind and brain, asking for and suggesting that same desired course of action. In either case, you are clearly indicating what would happen if it were up to you, putting your personal energy behind it, and asking the powers that be for their help.

You now have a method for reducing the stress that comes from unskillful handling of your bad worries. When you are ready to shift your focus to good worries—those that you may be able to do something about—go on to the next chapter, where I'll teach you how to make good worry even more effective.

7. Making Good Worry Better

You may be on the right track, but you'll get run over if you don't move.

—WILL ROGERS

Good worry is worry that focuses on a problem you may be able to do something about. Specific ways of both logical and emotional/intuitive thinking can help make you much more effective in resolving these issues or problems.

Greg was a twenty-eight-year-old college graduate who had been working for several years selling women's shoes in a large department store because he hadn't been able to find a job in advertising, his real area of interest. He'd looked for jobs in all the usual ways: reading the want ads, checking Craigslist, and enrolling in a number of online job search programs. He'd become depressed at times and given up looking for long periods. He constantly worried that he couldn't find a job in an area that could help him move into advertising.

When we went through the listing and sorting of worries, Greg thought about listing his job worries in the "cannot change" column, and I told him that he could park it there for a while but come back to it later if he wanted. He thought about it and then said, "No, I can't put it there. I have to do something to get started with an advertising career, no matter what it is."

Once Greg had chosen to classify this worry in his "can possibly change" column, I started him working on the Effective Action exercise I will teach you in this chapter. The first step was for Greg to clarify his goal. He wrote, "To work in advertising before the year is over." Then we went to the next step, generating ideas about how to accomplish this goal. After he had listed all the things he had already done without success, he went blank. I suggested that we go on an imaginary journey and talk to his inner wisdom figure to see how things looked from that perspective. He was surprised to find the image of a beaver industriously gnawing down small trees and building his dam. The beaver, while friendly enough, was intent on his work and answered questions while continuing to work. I suggested that Greg apologize for the interruption (manners go a long way even in imaginary conversations) but let the beaver know that he needed some help imagining how to get started in his own career. As the beaver kept gnawing and dragging and trimming and building his dam, he seemed to say that Greg should just get busy, start where he was, and not worry about whether he got paid or not. Greg told me, "He says that thinking about building a dam doesn't get it built. He has to actually cut down the trees and put them into the river, then weave them together and he has to use what he can find, and that's it. He says there's always stuff around to build with, even if it isn't ideal. I think he thinks that I should get busy and stop blaming it on the bad economy and bad job market, and move forward if that's really what I want to do."

In reviewing his imagery session, Greg realized that he had let the situation get him down. He had to think about whether advertising was important enough to him that he would do it for free with no guarantee of success. He realized that when he went to college he'd expected to get out, get hired by an established company, and work his way up the ladder until he had the position and success he wanted. Discovering that things didn't work like that anymore was difficult and discouraging. He saw that lots of people with established positions in advertising had lost their jobs as the economy suddenly contracted. To his advantage, though, he was young, he could live relatively inexpensively, and while he had little money, he had energy and creativity to invest in his future.

As Greg brainstormed about places he could volunteer his time, he realized that he could live on 80 percent of his current income and so could cut down to a four-day workweek. This gave him two or three days a week to volunteer and work creatively. He began to look for nonprofit agencies that could use some help and also started looking into Internet marketing, which wasn't something he (or anyone else) knew much about. He found a small company that was interested in selling its services over the Internet. Although they couldn't pay him at first, Greg helped the company create a new website that increased its sales significantly; after six months the company worked out a reimbursement agreement that more than made up for the income Greg had given up in his retail job. His new "partners" referred a couple of other small-business owners to him, and within another year he was able to quit his job and become a full-time Internet marketing consultant, which he loves.

Greg told me, "The beaver taught me to look around me, see what was there, and make use of it. I've come to feel that there are always opportunities sitting there unseen and unused because they aren't what I thought I was looking for. This realization has made me a more creative and confident person, and that's paying off for me in getting new clients. I'm getting hired now by some established companies and am really happy with my progress. My business is all mine and I feel great about that."

By bringing the creativity, perspective, and problem-solving abilities of his emotional and intuitive brain to the forefront, Greg found both the encouragement and motivation he needed to move forward. He also found that an unexpected solution (working for free) arose that had evaded his purely rational thought.

WHY DON'T WE AUTOMATICALLY RESOLVE THE ISSUES WE CAN DO SOMETHING ABOUT?

When we have a problem or worry that we can potentially do something about, there are a few common reasons for not making progress:

- We aren't really clear on what it is we want to do; we have left the issue so vague and uncertain that no goal can be set.
- We haven't been able to imagine a good way to accomplish what we want to accomplish, sometimes because we have become stuck in one way of thinking.
- We haven't really chosen the necessary course of ac-

tion, which prevents us from putting our energy and intention behind it.

- We haven't clearly delineated a plan that is likely to get us where we want to go.
- There are parts of us that have fears, concerns, or objections to resolving this problem and we haven't accounted for them.
- We need more motivation, courage, creativity, or other personal qualities to help us move out of our stuck place.

MAKING CHANGE HAPPEN: THE PROCESS OF EFFECTIVE ACTION

The Effective Action process addresses the issues listed above. It takes an idea that exists only in your mind and makes something real and tangible out of it. Effective Action is a refinement of the process I have referred to in my other books and audio programs as Turning Insight into Action, or Grounding. This is where the rubber meets the road, where things imagined become things with substance. This is the half of realizing your dreams that *The Secret* left out.

This is where you take the vision of your dream house, explain it to an architect, have plans drawn up, then give them to a contractor who actually buys the materials, hires and supervises the workers, and, after a lot of work, hands you the keys to a house that can actually keep you dry in a rainstorm, shelter and protect your family, and provide wall space where you can hang your art and family photos.

The Act of Will

Taking effective action is intimately connected with the will. For some people, once they know what they want, acting effectively to get it is second nature. Other folks may have great dreams but have trouble making them real. That is what the process of Effective Action planning is all about.

The will powers the process of moving from imagining something to actually doing something. Italian psychiatrist Roberto Assagioli, in his book *The Act of Will*, addressed the issues underlying people's failures to be successful in manifesting the changes they desire.

Assagioli found that when people had trouble effectively acting on their insights, they tended to break down or fall short in a specific step of activating the will. He thought that people tended to have a "weak link" in the chain of moving from insight to action, and that by looking at each component of the process, we could find out where it broke down, and address what needed to be strengthened in order to succeed. The steps he articulated address most of the pitfalls I mentioned earlier—failure to clarify our goals, generate suitable options, choose the best one, affirm our choices, or make and refine a plan. Let's look more closely at each component of taking effective action, and then we'll go through them as an exercise so you can address whichever of your "can possibly change" worries is most important.

Step One: Clarify Your Goal or Objective

The first step is to become as clear as possible about what you want to do. If you don't have a target, you aren't likely to hit it. Some people don't resolve their actionable worries because they are too vague about the goal, so their worries persist like unpulled weeds in the garden.

To clarify your goals, write them down in a short declarative sentence, and make that sentence as clear and unambiguous as it can possibly be. Include a timeline or deadline. Remember Greg? His goal was to be working in his chosen field within a year. Once he specified this goal, his creative energy began flowing in that direction. So will yours once you get clear on exactly what you want to do and set it as a goal.

STEP TWO: GENERATE OPTIONS

Sometimes people have a clear idea about what they want to accomplish but can't imagine how they will do it. That's the focus of this step—generating as many creative ideas as possible through a process popularly known as brainstorming. Greg was limited by his previous notion that he would get hired out of college by an established advertising agency or the marketing division of a company. When he realized that outcome was unlikely, he stopped looking for work. If he thought about it at all, he would get angry and depressed. After the unexpected "talk" with his imaginary beaver guide, he started to think creatively again, and in his brainstorming was able to open his mind to possibilities he hadn't thought of before.

Greg was interested to learn that the brainstorming approach was created by a prominent advertising leader named Alex Osborn in the 1930s; Osborn used it as a way to stimulate creativity and problem solving in groups. It can also be very effective when done individually if you follow some simple guidelines:

1. Defer judgment about your ideas. Postpone "reality test-ing" or any judgments about the quality of ideas until the process is over with.
2. Strive for quantity of ideas, not quality. Set a timer for ten minutes and just write down all the ideas that might help you attain your goal—the more the better.
3. Let yourself freewheel. Write down every idea, no matter how crazy, silly, or far afield, no matter whether they are legal, moral, affordable, or embarrassing. Encourage the free flow of ideas. Don't judge or analyze your ideas; you will take some time to sort them out later.

With solo brainstorming, the best approach is to take a big sheet of paper or a computer, set a timer for ten minutes, and write down every idea that comes to mind that can help you reach your goal. One idea tends to lead to another. Some idea-mapping software programs have built-in brainstorming timers for this purpose.

If you don't have many ideas, recruit some friends to help you. You could appoint a facilitator whose job is to encourage the flow of ideas and write them down as they come, or you can just ask people to write their ideas on Post-it notes and put them up on a wall or bulletin board. If you use a facilitator, he or she should encourage people to build on previous ideas but discourage discussion about why things will or won't work until the brainstorming session is over. Use the same guidelines dis-cussed above to keep new ideas flowing in the group.

Another option is to use guided imagery, asking your inner wisdom figure for its input. This will take more than ten min-utes and is best done as a separate exercise before or after the brainstorming session. Simply meditating for ten minutes or so before the brainstorming process can also make it easier to generate ideas if, for any reason, you have difficulty with the Inner Wisdom meditation.

While you will usually find a number of good options for action, it is also possible that brainstorming will make you realize that there isn't really much you can do about a particular worry. If that turns out to be the case, then reclassify it as a "cannot change" and either let it go or practice Positive Worry imagery with it.

STEP THREE: CHOOSE THE BEST OPTION

Once you've generated a lot of options, you'll need to sort them out and eliminate the ones that are silly, immoral, unaffordable, or otherwise impractical. Just cross them out as you look over your list. As you review the other possibilities, look for connections between ideas and for combinations that fit together well, and feel free to consolidate them into a single idea that serves your purpose. Sometimes while reviewing your options you may come up with other ideas, and that's fine; write them down, too. The whole point is to get to the best ideas.

When you've identified your best option, circle it, or write a new sentence that expresses *how* you will accomplish the goal you've identified in the first step of this process. Of course, you are also free to refine or modify your goal at any time.

How do you identify the "best" option? It should be the one that gives you the greatest chance of success. My friend and colleague Rachel Remen, M.D., says that the first thing to look for is the easiest option. The only caveat here is that the easy option must make enough of a difference to be significant.

At the Academy for Guided Imagery, a postgraduate training institute for health professionals, we adopted the guideline that the plan of action you choose should be "small enough to manage and big enough to matter." If your goal is to reduce your worrying about your weight by losing eighty pounds, you will probably find that overwhelming and depressing, but if you set that as your long-term goal and break it down into a series of smaller steps (for instance, aiming to lose five pounds in the first two weeks), you are much more likely to succeed. Choosing an action that can reward you with early success will help motivate you to take another manageable step, then another after that, and so on, until you reach your ultimate goal.

STEP FOUR: AFFIRM YOUR CHOICE

Now that you've chosen your best option, you'll want to see if you can put some real energy behind it. You can do that through the process of affirmation.

An affirmation states what you intend to do or be, and reminds you of your chosen goals. Affirmation is used to build motivation for taking the action steps you have identified, and to help you stay on course as you take whatever action is needed to be successful.

Begin by writing out a statement that starts with the phrase "I am . . . ," "I can . . . ," or "I will . . . ," and state clearly what it is you are going to do or be. Make your affirmation as straightforward and clear as possible. For instance, "I can lose five pounds in two weeks" is a simple affirmation. So is "I will eat only two-thirds of the food on my plate and skip desserts, except on Saturdays." One of my patients, a grandmother named Ruth, had as her goal "to worry less every day." Among the options generated in her brainstorming session was the idea that she could focus more on the present and less on the future. That's what she chose to concentrate on, and when she wrote out affirmations, the one that turned out to be most powerful for her was "I am aware of the preciousness of every moment." She used that statement as a mantra, a reminder of where she wanted to put her attention, and found that it helped her stay more in the present.

Once you've written out an affirmation that states what you will do or be, say it out loud. See if you can convince yourself that it is true. Repeat it again three to five times. If you can't put some significant energy into it by the fifth time you say it aloud, you may want to consider rewriting your affirmation until you have one you can believe in. If you can't convince yourself, you are very unlikely to be successful, so you are better off revising your goal and choice of action.

Once you've made a believer of yourself, you may want to share this affirmation with one or more people whom you consider your allies. Speaking affirmations aloud to others whom you respect and care for typically adds motivation and is a further test of your commitment to your chosen plan.

A good affirmation focuses your intention and your energy behind your choice. It is a statement that you can use to motivate yourself and keep yourself on track as you embark on your chosen action plan. An affirmation acts as a self-suggestion, too, reinforcing the new behavior in your brain. Use your affirmations frequently as guidelines, reminders, and motivators, especially early on. Write your affirmations on Post-it notes and stick them in places where you can't miss them—on the bathroom mirror, the dashboard of your car, your computer at work—so you will remember to reinforce your choice and encourage yourself along your way.

It's a good idea to repeat your affirmations to yourself very frequently, especially in the first five to seven days of acting on your plan. They get planted in your brain that way. I have known people who use affirmations as mantras, repeating them mentally hundreds of times a day until they feel well launched on their plan. This makes sense because you have to reinforce a new thought pattern frequently in order for it to become the default position.

Step Five: Make a Plan

Now that your direction is clear, write out a plan of action in as much detail as needed. Some plans can be quite simple, like Ruth's—she wrote out her affirmation and taped it to her bathroom mirror. The note reminded her every morning of her intention to bring her attention into each present moment.

Other plans require more detail. Our friend Greg's plan included researching and writing down a list of all the nonprofits in his area, researching Internet marketing and advertising online and at the library, creating a series of emails, letters, and Web-based messages that introduced him to various people and organizations, and creating a database of people he'd contacted and their responses.

One person's plan for weight loss included walking thirty minutes a day, avoiding restaurants that served food she couldn't resist, and immediately putting a third of the food on her plate into a carry-out box when she did eat out.

Write out your plan in enough detail so that it's easy to follow and all necessary steps are accounted for.

STEP SIX: REHEARSE YOUR PLAN WITH IMAGERY

Mentally rehearsing the successful execution of your plan is a very powerful way to review its thoroughness, affirm your choice, check for internal resistance, and build your motivation for following through. The most successful athletes, performance artists, and businesspeople routinely use imagery rehearsal. It is even used by both patients and doctors to speed surgeries and reduce the likelihood of complications.

Imagery rehearsal is a standard part of sports training now, especially at the higher levels of competition, where the mental game determines success as much or more than the physical characteristics of the competitors, who are all athletically gifted. In the early 1980s, visualization was not nearly as well known as it is now. A pair of twin brothers, Phil and Steve Mahre, dominated World Cup skiing during that time and won gold and silver medals for the United States at the 1984 Winter Olympics. A huge worldwide audience was introduced to imagery rehearsal as we watched the brothers close their eyes before each run and mentally go through every turn. You could see them making subtle body shifts and head movements as they vividly imagined what they wanted to do on their competitive runs.

Jack Nicklaus, still the greatest golfer of all, never hit a golf ball in competition without first mentally imagining where he wanted the ball to land, the trajectory he wanted the ball to take, and the swing he wanted to make. His competitors said that he was the best not because he had the best body but because he had the best mind.

Begin your imagery rehearsal by imagining carrying out each step of your plan, including what you will do, whom if anyone you will meet with, and what it will be like to reach a successful conclusion. There should be some kind of positive feeling at the end of your imagery. If there isn't, I'd question whether or not your goal is genuinely important to you. At the very least there should be a sense of relief, and preferably a positive feeling of accomplishment.

Imagery rehearsal is a powerful form of affirmation that brings your senses and feelings to bear on your motivation. By imagining what you see, hear, and feel as you go through your action plan, and especially by allowing yourself to really feel the emotional benefits of success, you create new associational pathways in your brain that pair those good feelings with the image of successfully carrying out your plan. You get to reap some of the emotional reward in advance, and that can help keep you focused and motivated as you work your plan.

Imagery rehearsal can also reveal gaps in your plan. Gina was twenty-six, a lovely young woman living on her own in San Francisco for the first time and worrying a lot about money. As she clarified her worries, she realized that she needed to (and could) greatly reduce her spending on clothes. She loved fashion but already had a huge wardrobe and could dress well without buying anything new for a good while. Her plan included budgeting a certain amount and only buying clothing on sale. As she imagined shopping downtown on Saturdays and going into all her favorite stores looking for sale items, she found herself imagining all the really nice new outfits that she was going to have to pass through in order to check out the items on sale. She saw, and felt, that it was going to be a real struggle for her, and decided that her plan needed to include limiting her shopping to only one Saturday a month, selling some of the clothing she never wore anymore, and finding some other fun but inexpensive things to do on the other weekend days.

STEP SEVEN: ACT ON YOUR PLAN

Once you've successfully imagined carrying out your plan and having the outcome you desire, it's time to act on it. Having done this mental preparation, you may discover that things will go smoothly for you. But real life has a way of throwing a monkey wrench into our best-laid plans, so you may run into unexpected obstacles. Don't freak out, and don't give up, either. Use the feedback you get from life as a way to further refine or adapt your plan to fit the circumstances.

Gina found that she missed her Saturday shopping days more than she expected to because it was something she did with a couple of her good girlfriends. After giving in to their entreaties and blowing too much money on a Saturday spree, she broke down crying. Her friends were concerned, and when she explained her situation, they all agreed that it would be better for all of them to do something more constructive and less expensive on their weekends. They listed a half dozen things they could enjoy doing together over the following Saturdays and vowed that when they did go clothes shopping they would be the savviest bargain hunters in the city.

That adjustment worked for Gina, but sometimes you will need to go back to the drawing board and completely revise your plan. If you do have to start over, carry your plan all the way through the imagery rehearsal step and then try it out again. Be flexible, adapt, experiment, and persevere. Remember that Thomas Edison went through more than twelve thousand failed experiments before he found the material that allowed him to invent a working lightbulb. Few of us have that kind of stick-to-it-iveness, but almost any change worth making deserves more than one or two tries.

Now that I've explained the Effective Action process, it's

time for you to try it out on one of your "can possibly change" worries.

Preparing for Your Effective Action Planning Process

The process of grounding—turning insight into action—is something you may or may not do well instinctively. Unlike the other processes you have learned, this one will be broken down into steps and be done mostly with your eyes open. You'll write down answers to questions about what you want to change and how you will go about it. Each step is important, and if you go through the process step by step, you will end up with a plan that is likely to bring you success.

Take as long as you need with each step. This can be a process you complete in a single session of forty-five minutes or one that you'll work with over several days or even longer until you have a plan that suits you.

Before you begin, make sure you have writing materials, a ten-minute timer, and a comfortable place where you can close your eyes and do guided imagery rehearsal when the time comes. There's no need to do deep relaxation until you reach the stage of mental rehearsal. At that point you can go through it on your own, have someone read you the script, or use my audio recording (www.worrysolution.com) to lead you through the process.

EFFECTIVE ACTION PLANNING

Clarify Your Insight

Take some time to state to yourself as clearly and simply as you can what you want to do. Write down the clearest sentence you can that expresses what you wish to act on. Take some time to carefully look at the sentence you've written, making sure that there are no extra words and that it states clearly what you would like to take action on.

Take some time to carefully look at the sentence you've written and decide which word is most important. Look at each word carefully. Make sure that it's just the right word to express exactly what you mean, and take as much time as you need to do this.

Generate Options (Brainstorming)

Next, think about this statement and list all the possible ways you might practically accomplish this goal. Brainstorm about this. Take a large sheet of paper, set a timer for ten minutes, and write down as many ways as you can think of that would be a step in this direction. Don't edit as you write. Just let yourself list all the possibilities and ideas that come to mind, whether or not they're realistic, affordable, ethical, or legal. Write down every idea that comes to mind that might help you take a step in the direction of grounding your insight. Go for quantity. Invite your unconscious mind and/or your inner wisdom figure to contribute any and all ideas.

Choose the Best Option

Now take some time to look over your options. Look at all the things you've written down and other things that may come to mind as you review them, and notice if you can combine any ideas. Eliminate any that are unethical, illegal, unaffordable, or otherwise unsuitable, and focus on the ones that likely would be most successful. Give consideration to any that would be the most practical for you to actually carry out and that would be the easiest to act on, as long as they would result in success.

Is there one way that promises the most success or the greatest return for the least effort? Make sure the option you choose is big enough to matter but small enough to manage. And when you're ready, choose the option that seems the best for you and circle that choice on your list, or write it out in another sentence that says what you've chosen to do.

Affirmation

Write an affirmation statement about your choice that starts with "I will ...," "I am ...," or "I can ..."

Listen to yourself as you say your affirmation out loud. It'll give you an idea of how much energy and commitment you can really put behind this choice. You may feel awkward at first, but repeat it several times and you should find yourself being able to put a wholehearted commitment behind it. If you can't state your intention aloud and convince yourself that it is something you can and will do, you may want to consider making another choice that you can more authentically affirm.

Write an Action Plan

Now write down a concrete plan for carrying out your choice of actions. Consider what specific steps are involved and in what order you need to take them. Whom might you have to speak to and what might you need to do? Make a specific plan in simple yet detailed steps, and write down your plan, making sure it is clear and practical. Take all the time you need to do this. The better you plan, the more likely your success. Writing down your plan is the first time your idea comes into a physical form, and it turns a holistic, multifaceted idea into a project that requires sequential action steps.

Imagery Rehearsal

Now you can rehearse your plan, in detail, in your imagination. Get comfortable, close your eyes, and take a couple of deep, full breaths, inviting your body to relax and to release any tension it doesn't need to hold, breathing in fresh energy and oxygen on the in-breath, releasing tension or distraction on the out-breath, inviting your body to be at ease and to be comfortable. And as you breathe gently and easily, allow your mind to become quiet and still...

And as you breathe, you may want to go to your special inner place and become comfortable there, noticing what you see there today, what you imagine hearing, what the air is like, what time of day or night it seems to be, what the temperature is like, and especially how it feels to be there, and finding the spot where you feel most relaxed yet most aware and centered, letting yourself get comfortable there...

And when you're ready, imagine yourself actually carrying out your plan. Use your imagination to see and feel yourself carrying out your plan from start to finish, to give yourself a sense of what may happen in real life. Begin at the beginning, imagining yourself carrying out the action you've chosen, all the way through to the successful conclusion...

As you do this, notice which parts of your plan seem easy, and which parts may be harder...And as you imagine carrying out your plan, you may become aware of issues or obstacles that you didn't think of before. These may be events, people, or simply your own feelings and attitudes that arise as you begin to think about acting on your plan. If obstacles appear that you didn't account for, simply think about how you'll adjust your plan to take them into consideration. This is the easiest and least expensive place to adjust your plan, so take the time needed and be thankful for every resource and barrier that you anticipate...

You might find that you need to change your plan or adjust it, or break it down into smaller steps to make it happen...Take all the time you need to adjust your plan until you can imagine yourself carrying it out successfully...

When you're able to imagine carrying out your plan successfully, you should feel some kind of positive feeling at the end. It may be as mild as a sense of relief, or there may be a sense of pride, accomplishment, or joy, some positive feeling that comes along with successfully carrying out your plan. Let yourself feel that positive feeling, and notice where you feel it in your body. And if you like, you can invite that feeling to become larger and stronger within you ...

Imagine that it grows and begins to radiate out, going to all parts of your body and mind. You might even imagine you have a control, like you do on a radio or television, and you can turn that positive feeling up as strong as you like. Imagine it penetrating deeply to the core of your being, and filling you up, all the way out to the outermost cells of your skin, and beyond ... letting yourself just enjoy that positive feeling as deeply and fully as you can experience it right now ...

You've imagined taking an action, and you've followed it through successfully, and now you can enjoy the positive feeling that comes with that ...

And once you've enjoyed those positive feelings for a bit, take the time to go back to the beginning of your plan and imagine carrying it through again to a successful conclusion, feeling that positive feeling again, perhaps even more strongly ... And let yourself do this two or three more times until you can easily envision yourself carrying out your plan successfully and feeling this positive feeling at its conclusion ...

You may want to take additional time to rehearse your plan in your imagination again and again. The more you do this, the easier it will be to follow through on your plan, and the positive feeling that you feel at the end will help to motivate and sustain you as you work through any issues or obstacles that may arise.

Now when you are ready, let the images go and prepare to open your eyes and come back to the outer world, bringing with you whatever's important, including this positive feeling that you've experienced and the inner success you've had in carrying out your plan already…When you come all the way back to the outer world you can open your eyes, gently stretch, and as you come wide awake and refreshed, take some time to write about any changes or adjustments you've made in your plan, about any obstacles you've anticipated and how you might deal with them if they arise, and about how it felt to imagine yourself successfully completing your plan…

Acting on Your Plan

Finally it's time to take your plan out for a test drive. Stay aware of what is working and what needs adapting or modifying in your plan as you proceed. Sometimes you may need to loop back and make a change to account for something that didn't turn up in your planning or your imagery. Remember what they say about the best-laid plans, stay flexible, and have confidence in your ability to adapt or problem-solve when you need to in order to keep moving toward your target goal.

Like a sailor planning a trip from port to port, you may find that sometimes the winds change directions and you need to tack back and forth to make gains. Some of the time it may not seem like you are heading directly to your destination, but if you keep your eye on where you want to go as you alter course, that will get you there most quickly.

If you need to change your plans to account for an unanticipated barrier, you may find it helpful to go back through whichever earlier steps are necessary to repeat. You may need to restate or clarify your goal once again, brainstorm new possibilities, or make another choice and modify your plan so that you achieve your goals.

Reviewing Your Effective
Action Planning Process

Take a few moments to think about, and maybe write about, what you noticed as you worked through this process.

What seemed most important or significant to you?

Did you learn anything valuable as you went through this process?

Are there any additional resources you need in order to achieve your objectives? If so, where might you find them, and how would you use them?

How confident do you feel about being successful with this plan? What would make you even more confident?

You may want to take the time to go inside and consult with your inner wisdom if you get stuck at any point, to make sure that you are making room for all of your intelligence to participate in helping you succeed.

You now have a number of powerful skills in your Worry Solution tool kit. You have ways to calm yourself and quiet your mind, a way to connect with the wisdom of your emotional/ intuitive brain, a way to transform "bad" habitual worry, and a way to be more effective in changing things that are possible to change. While you experiment with these software upgrades, let's take a look at what science says this may have to do with the hardware of your brain.

8. Minding Your Brain

Swiftly the brain becomes an enchanted loom, where millions of flashing shuttles weave a dissolving pattern—always a meaningful pattern—though never an abiding one.

—SIR CHARLES SHERRINGTON

What is the relationship between the mind and the brain? Is the mind an epiphenomenon of the brain, a by-product that develops when the neuronal architecture of the brain is complex enough to allow it to become aware of itself? Or is the mind a primary force that uses the brain and body to accomplish its purposes in life?

The short answer is that nobody knows. We do know that the mind and brain are so intertwined that it behooves us to understand more about both. For our purposes here, it's useful to think of the brain and mind like the hardware and software of a computer—they are intricately interdependent and neither one is much use without the other. If we use this simple model, we could consider the Worry Solution program to be a software upgrade that will make your brain hardware more efficient and user-friendly. Whether worry originates in the brain or mind, whether it is a hardware or software problem, the brain clearly provides the physical pathways that signal the body to respond by either taking action, letting go, or stewing in its own "worry juices."

The adult human brain weighs about three to four pounds, and most of that is fat. Men, on average, have somewhat larger brains than women, and in this case, it really isn't the size that counts—it's how you use it. Surprisingly, humans don't have the biggest brains on earth, not even relative to body size. An elephant's brain is six times bigger than that of a human, and a bottlenose dolphin's is about the same size. The mouse has three times the ratio of brain size to body size. Yet we have a type of intelligence that the other creatures do not, perhaps as a result of the complex interconnected nerve networks in specific brain areas that have allowed us to develop speech, mathematics, and symbolic and abstract reasoning.

Whether the unique kind of thinking humans have developed is a good thing or not remains to be seen. While we are clever and inventive, it isn't yet clear that we have the wisdom to use our intelligence in a sustainable way. Douglas Adams, author of *A Hitchhiker's Guide to the Universe,* writes, "Man has always assumed that he was more intelligent than dolphins because he had achieved so much—the wheel, New York, wars and so on—while all the dolphins had ever done was muck about in the water having a good time. But conversely, the dolphins have always believed that they were far more intelligent than man—for precisely the same reason."

Brain size in humans varies a good deal and does not directly correlate with intelligence. A gifted person considered to be a genius was found to have a brain weighing only two pounds, while one of the highest recorded brain weights (six pounds) belonged to a man with severe mental retardation.

The brain contains somewhere between 11 billion and 30 billion neurons (nerve cells) and ten times as many support cells, called glia. Each nerve cell has approximately 10 million synapses (direct connections with other nerve cells), and the amount of information flowing through this network (a minimum of 100 quadrillion—that's 100,000,000,000,000,000—connections) is almost unimaginable. Because of the tremendous flow of energy through this immensely active network, the brain, which accounts for only 2 to 3 percent of body weight, uses 20 to 25 percent of all the energy produced in the body.

We know where many functions are physically located in the brain, although the connections between these areas also have a lot to do with how the brain ultimately works. The speech centers are normally found in specific regions of the left brain, while the body image is in a similar location in the right brain; vision is mostly processed in the occipital lobes in the rear of the brain, and hearing along the sides in the temporal lobes. Fear and anger are modulated in a part of the emotional brain known as the amygdala, and significant experiences are routed through the hippocampus to be placed in long-term memory. Thirst, hunger, and sleep patterns are regulated in the hypothalamus, a tiny center at the base of the brain that, depending on the information it receives from the rest of the brain, sends either alarm or all-clear signals to the body. Planning, judgment, and decision-making functions largely reside behind the forehead, in the prefrontal cortex, especially on the left side, whereas spatial relationships and emotional recognition are more the province of the right side of the cortex.

Is the Mind in the Brain?

In spite of all that we know about the brain, we still do not know where the mind itself lives. I'm not even sure we know what a mind is. Most neuroscientists, including my colleague David Bresler, Ph.D., at the Academy for Guided Imagery, say that it has a lot to do with where we place our attention.

Being able to notice and choose where you focus your attention is a large part of what makes human consciousness so powerful. The choices you make (or don't make) about where you put your attention may determine the quality of your daily life more than any other choices you make.

The ability to choose what you do with your attention is both the great opportunity and the great challenge of being human. We can either be mindless or mindful; we can be of two minds about something; we can make up our minds; we can choose to mind our own business or that of others, mind our manners, or give someone a piece of our mind. We can even choose to believe that our choices create our reality or that our choices are illusionary. We can choose to believe that life is random and meaningless or that it has a purpose and order. These choices make a huge difference in how we experience ourselves and our lives.

Still, we don't exactly know what a mind is. And maybe we don't have to know exactly what it is or where it is. Just because we can't exactly define it or find it in the fat, folds, and bumps of the brain doesn't mean that we can't learn to use our minds more effectively. We know that brain and mind, like thinking and feeling, are intimately intertwined and that they can both be sources of and antidotes for worry.

What Can Brain Development Teach Us About Worry?

Over time, in both evolution and personal development, we see that the brain has continually added new abilities to its repertoire. Looking back across the timeline of life, we see the first appearance of nerve cells in jellyfish and a primitive brain in the flatworm. The worm brain is simply a large congregation of nerve cells near the sensory organs in the head. With the increased density of intertwining neurons comes increasingly complex information processing.

As animals grew more complicated than worms, they developed larger and more complex brains. The brain acts like the central processing unit (CPU) of a computer. It receives input from our senses and our memories, and after comparing the present data to past experiences, it activates programs aimed at helping us to survive, thrive, and reach our goals.

Different species have preferentially developed different brain areas that allow them to exploit different niches in the environment—birds can fly and gophers can dig—but in general they also retain the brain structures that have already developed in creatures before them. That way, each species benefits from the adaptations that have proven useful to earlier organisms. The early brain functions that aided survival in fish, lizards, birds, and other primates persist in the human brain, and on top of these capabilities we have developed new areas that let us imagine how the future might be and allow us to plan so that we can avoid dangers and take advantage of opportunities.

A side effect of this ability to "time-travel" in our imaginations is that we can also worry. If we aren't careful, we can worry ourselves sick or to distraction. Learning more about how the brain is organized will help you understand why and how the Worry Solution "software upgrades" can be so beneficial.

THE TRIUNE BRAIN

The great Yale psychiatrist and neuroscientist Paul D. MacLean first described his evolutionary model of the triune brain in the 1950s. MacLean described three major brain levels that operate like "three interconnected biological computers, [each]

The Triune Brain

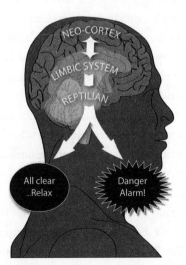

with its own special intelligence." While the brain is now un-derstood to be more complex than that, the three-level divi-sion is still a useful working model in helping us to understand how we worry, and how we can worry less.

The hindbrain, the most ancient part of our brain, sits at the top of the spinal cord and regulates basic functions such as hunger, thirst, sexual desire, body temperature, and sleep cycles. Commonly referred to as the "reptilian brain," this area is mostly concerned with helping us avoid things that might eat us, and finding things that we can eat or mate with. It responds directly and reflexively to what it senses in the environment, does not feel or process emotion, and doesn't assign meaning to events or think about them at all. If you give this primitive brain a safe, warm place to be, something good to eat, and another of its kind to copulate with, it's happy. Many female readers may think this description applies to their husbands, boyfriends, or males in general. The reason will become clear when we look at the emotional, or "limbic" brain, the next level of brain evolution.

The limbic system, which we share with other mammals, receives and processes information that is more complex than that in the reptile brain. The limbic brain is primarily concerned with emotional processing and the status of our emotional relationships. It is the part of the brain that is re-sponsible for wolf packs, gorilla families, mother-child bond-ing, marriages, and feelings of affinity for others. Emotional intelligence depends a great deal on these limbic areas of the brain, and women are generally more sophisticated and skilled than men in this important arena of life.

Studies show that women have three or four times the amount of brain area devoted to emotionally important func-tions than men do. They are better than men at recognizing emotions in facial expression, tone of voice, and body posture, and have a much greater capacity to use emotionally relevant language. In fact, one of the most important effects of testosterone in the developing male fetus and male adolescent is to kill off neurons in the area of the brain responsible for emotionally charged communication. Anyone who has known a sweet teenage boy who disappears into his room for a couple of years at fourteen or fifteen and then emerges as a different person has witnessed the real-life aspects of this transformation.

It isn't that men don't have their own emotional intelligence, but it does seem that nature has deemphasized this ability in males, apparently to free up brain space for territoriality, aggressiveness, and sexuality. These are primary areas of importance to the male brain, ensuring that men procreate, feed, and protect their genetic line. These traditionally male concerns support the survival of the species by making it more likely that the strongest, most dominant genes are passed on. With considerably less brain space devoted to emotional processing, men may miss emotional cues and nuances that are obvious to their female friends, mates, and lovers. They are simply not as well equipped to notice these as women.

In both genders, the cerebral cortex, the "thinking cap" that sits on top of the other two brain divisions, is the largest part of the brain. This third and highest level of the brain, sometimes called the neocortex, is where perception is processed to form visual, auditory, and kinesthetic (tactile) images, and where judgments, meanings, and stories about these impressions are formed. These interpretations and attributions create a unique reality for each of us, one that is not simply a result of what we see, hear, and feel, but is modified by our previous experiences, preferences, psychological defenses, and emotional tolerances. As far as we know, this kind of story making is another uniquely human ability. The ways we have learned to think about life from our past experiences tend to perpetuate themselves and influence how we process what happens next. That's how we get stuck in bad mental habits.

I know two people who have won sizable amounts of money in lotteries. Jennie reacted with the joy you'd expect—excited about the win, the money, and all the possibilities it opened up for her. Walter got very anxious, saying, "Oh crap. Now I'll have to pay a ton of taxes and everybody I know is going to be after me for something." It made me wonder why he bought a ticket. The point is, the same thing happens to two people and they have very different experiences because they run different stories about the event in their minds.

In this case, the sudden life change precipitated by the lottery win triggered excitement in Jennie's emotional brain but fear in Walter's. The emotional signal went up to the cortex and thoughts, images, and memories were woven together in a way that produced predictions. The signals resulting from the stories that were created in each of their thinking brains traveled back down through the emotional and reptile brains, where they activated different reactions. In Walter's case, his fears created enough stress and anxiety that he needed to take antianxiety medicine for a while. The fear and worry set up a reverberating circuit that continuously reinforced itself. Over time, with support from his family and some cognitive therapy, Walter was able to appreciate his good fortune and interpret his win differently. As his inner narrative changed about this event, his cortex sent different signals down through his emotional and reptilian brains and he was able to calm down and discontinue his medication.

We have little control over our initial emotional and instinctive reactions because they travel on a "fast pathway" designed by nature to immediately get us out of dangerous situations or to pursue fleeting opportunities. But soon after those initial responses, the cortex gets involved, analyzing and creating stories about our experiences. These stories can alter the way we then respond emotionally, and that's where learning to use our brains more consciously can help us. We can reprogram our brains by reimagining and rewriting some of the stories that live unconsciously in our cortex, and those rewrites can change the way we feel about some of the things that worry us.

EACH BRAIN LEVEL AFFECTS THE OTHERS

The three brain divisions are intricately interconnected, and impulses at each level often affect the other two. Thus someone or something may attract or repel us at an emotional or even instinctual level, and later we will try to rationalize and explain that feeling. Advertisers are well aware of this "bottom-up" motivational pathway and design ads that are aimed at first engaging the emotional brain. They know that if there is a strong emotional attraction to an ad, the attractive images and the product may be tied together in the brain. When the emotional brain likes what it sees, the logical brain will often find a reason to justify a purchase. That's why pretty girls dominate beer ads, beautiful women hock cosmetics, and happy-looking people sell products ranging from pharmaceuticals to automobiles.

Your thinking and feeling brain divisions are not always in agreement, and conflicts about purchases are a good everyday example. Have you ever really wanted something like a fabulous pair of shoes, a piece of jewelry, or a sports car, where you just had to have it even though you knew it was way too expensive or impractical for you? Did you agonize about the purchase, going back and forth between the reasons that tell you no and the craving that tells you yes? That was a conversation between your thinking brain and your feeling brain.

The emotional decision takes only twelve milliseconds, while the rational decision takes twice as long. Once the emotional brain has decided it wants something, it takes a lot of rational argument to change its mind. That's why the advertisers target the emotional brain first.

If our thinking and feeling brains are in agreement, we buy or don't buy, we go out with the guy or not, we stay in our job or leave it, and life is congruent and relatively simple. When our reason and emotion disagree, however, we find ourselves uncomfortable and conflicted. It turns out that in those situations we aren't just of two minds about the issue; we are probably of two brains about it as well.

The Emotional Brain Has a Cortex, Too

The terms "right brain" and "left brain" have almost become clichés over the past forty years. While it is an oversimplification to assign all logical thought to the left brain and all intuitive and symbolic thought to the right, the distinction is another useful metaphor. There are indeed significant differences in the way that different brain regions process information. Research on patients who have had the two sides of their brain separated (split-brain subjects) confirms that both hemispheres are highly intelligent, with the right brain more closely integrated with imagery and emotions and the left side more specialized for speech and logic.

In 1981 Roger Sperry, a neuroscientist at the California Institute of Technology, received the Nobel Prize for demonstrating that we actually have two brains—or, more accurately, that both sides of the cerebral cortex are individually capable of high-level information processing. Our cerebral cortex is divided in half, looking quite a bit like an oversized walnut, with the two halves (hemispheres) wired together by large bundles of nerve pathways.

In early research, Sperry introduced lab monkeys to a light board that flashed random sequences of numbers, and the monkeys quickly learned that if they touched the numbers in the same order, they would be rewarded with food. Sperry then surgically disconnected the two hemispheres of the monkeys' brains, meaning that he was able to send the lighted number sequences to only one side or the other. When the numbers were sent to the left side of a monkey's brain, its right hand responded (each hemisphere controls the opposite side of the body) and punched in the proper sequences. When the numbers were sent to the right side of a monkey's brain, its left hand performed the task just as well.

When Sperry sent two different sequences at the same time to the two disconnected sides of the monkey's brain, its left and right hands operated independently, simultaneously punching in both number sequences. It was as if there were two monkey brains in each of these split-brain monkey bodies, and each brain hemisphere proved equally capable of learning complex tasks. In normal monkeys with connected hemispheres, only one side of the brain could answer at a time, and in most cases the dominant left brain and right hand responded, inhibiting the response of the subdominant right hemisphere.

Dr. Joseph Bogen, a neurosurgeon colleague of Sperry's, noticing that the laboratory monkeys survived this surgical separation without any apparent neurological problems, began researching a similar operation in an attempt to save the lives of a number of human patients suffering from life-threatening epilepsy. None of the usual medications had worked for these patients, and they were in serious danger of dying from prolonged seizures. Bogen's hope was that by separating the two hemispheres, the seizure activity could at least be limited to one side of the brain and body, which would allow the patients to continue to breathe and hence survive their seizures. Fortunately, the operation was even more successful than anticipated, and in the forty-one patients who had this procedure, all but one became completely free of seizure activity. Even more remarkably, once the patients recovered from the surgery, they seemed unchanged to their families, friends, and examining doctors.

What's truly amazing about this outcome is that in order to separate the sides of the brain, Bogen had to completely sever the corpus callosum, a huge information highway of nerve fibers that connects the two sides of the brain. The corpus callosum normally transmits as many as 5 billion nerve impulses every second between the hemispheres—a lot of information flow to interrupt without any apparent change in behavior or personality.

Fortunately for our understanding of brain function, many of these patients volunteered to be tested by Dr. Sperry. In one experiment, the subjects sat at a table and reached under a screen to handle a variety of common objects they couldn't see. Sperry had them focus their gaze on a spot directly in front of them and then flashed a word for a tenth of a second at the extreme right or left of their visual field, thus sending the message to only one side of the brain at a time.

Movies of these experiments are stunning. When a subject—

let's call him Joe—receives the message "comb" in his left brain, his right hand goes under the screen, touches a pen, a watch, and a book, and then finds the comb and holds it up. The experimenter asks him what happened and Joe answers, "I saw the word *comb,* and I searched through some other stuff until I found the comb and held it up."

Then the word *pen* is flashed to Joe's right brain. His left hand immediately goes under the screen and examines the various objects until he finds and holds up the pen. Joe is asked what happened, and replies, "Huh? Nothing. I'm just waiting for the next message." Joe has no idea that a message was sent or received, and no awareness that his left hand not only moved but also accurately found the object in question and held it up for display. Something intelligent was at work, but Joe wasn't aware of it.

In another experiment, Joe is flashed pictures to both sides of the brain simultaneously. His left brain sees a picture of a hammer and the right brain a picture of a handsaw. The experimenter asks him what he saw, and Joe says, "Hammer." He is then asked to close his eyes and let his left hand (connected to his right brain) draw what he saw—and he draws the handsaw. When Joe looks at the picture, he recognizes that it's a drawing of a saw, but when he's asked why he drew it, he has no idea. You can watch a video of this experiment and others like it on YouTube (www.youtube.com/watch?v=ZMLzP1VCANo). They are stunning to watch.

Through this and many other elegant experiments, Sperry's team found that "Joe" actually lived in his left brain, and that the named self that we all identify with is inextricably tied to our ability to talk and name things. When our hemispheres are surgically separated, our right brain demonstrates itself to be highly intelligent and even better than our left brain at certain tasks, such as understanding emotional body language, facial expressions, and tones of voice. Its speech ability is quite limited, though, and if its thoughts and feelings are going to be put into words, the information needs to be sent across the corpus callosum to the left brain's speech centers. Once there, it may be directly expressed, but it can also be altered, edited, suppressed, or even ignored. The exceptions to this are some commonly used idioms and swearing, an especially direct way of expressing emotion.

So now we have two large areas of the cortical brain that process and express themselves in different ways, one through facial expression, body language, and tone of voice, and the other in words. The right brain can also express itself in drawing, painting, singing, dance, music, and other expressive arts. The two sides of the brain, like the emotional and rational brains, can be in agreement about what is important, or they can be in conflict. When they conflict, the so-called dominant left hemisphere often "wins," at least temporarily, because it can superimpose an interpretation, a narrative, or even a lie on top of the more unprocessed, unedited, and less verbal state.

The dominant hemisphere is on the left in the vast majority of people, even if they are left-handed, which means that our primary speech centers are located there. Our speech centers are what let us conceptualize and describe ourselves as unique identities, a big step in achieving self-consciousness. They let me say, "Hi, I'm Marty Rossman, I'm from Detroit, Michigan, but I now live in northern California, and I've been a doctor for nearly forty years." You would have some similar description of who you were and where you live and what you do. If we don't look any deeper, we would think that this description sums up who we are. But that would be a mistake, because while we are all those things, we are also much more.

Our ability to think rationally and to use speech and numbers has allowed us to build on our imaginative abilities and emerge as the most dominant creatures on earth. Perhaps because of this evolutionarily new and astounding power to alter our environment, the left brain has become a little over-impressed with itself. Because it alone has the ability to name things, it calls itself the dominant or major hemisphere. That's fair, because it can and does provide an override function in relation to the more emotional right brain, but it makes a serious mistake when it thinks that it is the *only* hemisphere that counts. While logical thinking is necessary for building skyscrapers and flying to the moon, it is nearly useless when it comes to creating and maintaining an emotionally intimate relationship or responding to fast-developing threats.

The split-brain research showed us that we have another type of intelligence that coexists with our usual way of think-ing about and describing our world. This intelligence has its own perspective, priorities, form of information processing, and motivations. It influences our daily lives much more than we know. This intelligent unconscious mind undoubtedly lives not only in the right brain but also in other areas of both brain hemispheres and in parts of the limbic brain that lack direct access to speech. It has eons of evolutionary experience that can guide us or help us solve problems. It tends to think in terms of how things are connected, rather than how they are different, and it excels in recognizing both spatial and social relationships. Bringing this emotional/intuitive intelligence into our problem solving and emotional coping efforts greatly expands our ability to worry well; it lets us use all of our brain capacity to resolve worry and stress rather than create them.

The key to connecting with this rich inner intelligence is first quieting the rational brain so that we can also become aware of the subtler, imagery-laden thoughts that carry the messages of our silent, emotional, and intuitive brains. That simple act of respect adds a tremendous amount of experience, wisdom, and brainpower to our deliberations and decisions, and in difficult situations we can use all the brainpower we can get.

So What Does This All Mean for the Worry Solution Approach?

The ways that the different parts of our brains process information, and the fact that the thinking and emotional divisions of our brains can each arouse, stimulate, or calm the other, can help us understand how to use each to reduce or resolve worry.

To simplify what we have learned about the brain: the limbic areas, the reptilian brain, and the right hemisphere together constitute what we might call the emotional/intuitive brain, while the left hemisphere contains what we can call the thinking brain. The emotional and intuitive parts of the brain are less amenable to direct change than the thinking areas because they react more quickly and instinctively to what they fear and desire. The thinking brain is where you can have the most effect. Considering alternative interpretations of the signals that the emotional/intuitive brain sends up to your thinking brain is the primary way you can modify the actions and reactions you have to things that bother or worry you.

Because the way we think about things that worry us is often determined by long habit, entertaining new thoughts and perspectives can often be the key to bypassing or replacing old patterns of feeling and behavior. One of the interesting qualities of imagery is that it can usually be interpreted in a num-

ber of different ways. Years ago I had a patient who was quite
ill. She wanted very badly to live and was desperately trying to
use mind/body medicine to physically heal herself. One day
an image of God came to her, in which he was standing on a
bridge and reaching out his hand to her. She heard the message that it was safe to cross and that he would always be with
her. I became a bit alarmed because I read it as a sign that
she was getting close to dying. She, however, experienced it as
a very reassuring message, and it relieved her of a great deal
of anxiety. Her feeling and thinking brains "agreed" on the
meaning of this image, and it put many of her fears to rest.

How Your Brain Creates Your Personal Reality

Barbara was an attractive middle-aged divorced woman with
many friends. Smart, funny, and gregarious, she was a charmer
whom people naturally enjoyed being around, and she had a
wide circle of admiring men as well as girlfriends with whom
she frequently socialized. In spite of her popularity, Barbara
lacked confidence about her relationships. She would torture
herself after almost every conversation she had, worrying about
whether she had offended someone or said something stupid
or whether the person really liked her. She would agonize over
calling someone back to apologize for something she'd said or
done, regardless of whether she'd really done anything insult-
ing or offensive. She was highly anxious, had trouble sleeping,
had been in therapy for years, took tranquilizers, and drank a
fair amount of alcohol besides.

Somewhere in her brain circuitry she lacked a sense of confidence about how others viewed her, and an internal alarm about this stimulated her to compulsively review possible scenarios of what might have gone wrong and how she could fix it. If we could look at Barbara's brain with an fMRI when she was worrying, would we see that the distress originated in her thinking brain or in her feeling brain? Did she *think* that somehow she wasn't good enough, smart enough, or pretty enough to rate well with others, which then stimulated anxious feelings, or did her emotional brain *feel* that she was in danger of getting cut off and left alone, which prompted her thinking brain to try to understand what changes she might need to make to stay a part of the group? It could be either or both. Knowing which comes first isn't as important as understanding that she has the ability to change her thinking and feeling patterns to ones that are true for her but more comfortable to live with.

Once she was in a relaxed but focused state, I asked Barbara to invite an image to come to mind that could tell her something helpful about this issue. She was surprised when a large multifaceted crystal ball appeared, "kind of like a disco ball," she said. The ball rotated slowly, reflecting light off its many facets. As she looked at the mirrorlike surfaces she saw different images of herself and felt many different emotions. In one facet she saw herself as a lonely child who spent a lot of solitary time in her room while her parents were out socializing; in another she appeared as a teenager worrying about her skin and whether her breasts would develop to look like those of the other girls; in a third she was an adult enjoying a party with many friends; and in yet another she appeared as a happy young mother holding her own daughter in her arms. There were many other images of her reflected in other facets of the ball.

As she observed this image she suddenly said, "You know, I am all of this. I can be happy and content or anxious and lonely. I get the sense that I could actually pick and choose the way I'd like to be, if I wanted to." As she continued to watch the ball turn, she got the sense that other people were also like mirrors in that they reflected different aspects of herself back to her and influenced which of her many facets became prominent.

The mirror imagery was very powerful for Barbara. She talked about how changing the angle she took in relation to the mirrors actually changed the way she looked. She started to see how she could change the way she related to some people and situations, and saw that she had much more choice in that than she had previously realized. She also saw that drinking too much interfered with her ability to make choices about which parts of herself to reveal or emphasize. She saw that drinking made her vulnerable to regrets the next day since she didn't always remember all the interactions she'd had the night before.

Barbara found that she could start to consciously use the reflecting ball to "light up" the parts of herself that she wanted to display or share with others. In her therapy, she became less concerned with how she'd gotten to be the way she was and more focused on how she could become more the way she wanted to be. Being able to make choices about which qualities she emphasizes has helped Barbara feel more in control, more confident, and quite a bit less concerned about the opinions of others.

As Barbara developed the practice of meditating on the way she preferred to be in various social situations, she became noticeably less anxious about them. She drank very little and after several months was able to stop the regular use of medications for anxiety. Barbara had changed the way she used her mind, and while we didn't do any brain scans on her, she almost certainly changed long-established patterns in her brain.

The Brain's Remarkable Ability to Change

In the past fifteen or twenty years we have learned that the brain learns and changes throughout life, can repair itself to a much greater degree than was previously thought possible, and that some areas of the brain can take over functions lost through damage to other areas. The degree to which the brain can change and adapt is the most surprising and important finding of what neuroscientists have learned about the brain in recent years.

In *The Brain That Changes Itself*, Columbia University psychiatrist Norman Doidge describes people who have been blind since birth learning to see well enough to walk around strange rooms by themselves, avoiding obstacles as if they were sighted. They manage this feat by wearing tiny video cameras that send them visual information translated into small electrical signals conveyed to them through their back or tongue. Remarkably, the part of their brain that would normally process visual information from the eyes takes this new tactile input and processes it in a way that gives them a type of vision. Doidge describes many other examples of people who regain other lost or absent functions when their brains can be provided with the right kind of stimuli.

The key message that Doidge has popularized is that the brain is able to learn new patterns even after parts of it have been destroyed or unused for long periods. This research is encouraging for those of us who want to learn new skills and patterns of thinking; it shows us that, with practice, we can change not only our minds but also our brains.

CAN WE CHANGE OUR WORRYING BRAINS BY CHANGING OUR MINDS?

Some of the research that is most directly relevant to the Worry Solution approach comes from the laboratory of Dr. Jeffrey Schwartz, coauthor of *The Mind and the Brain* and an associate professor of psychiatry at UCLA. Schwartz has found that people with severe obsessive-compulsive disorder (OCD) can create new pathways in the brain that begin to free them from compulsive reactions after only ten weeks of practice. Historically, OCD has been an extremely difficult form of mental illness to treat; medications and various forms of psychotherapy have met with only limited success.

People with OCD suffer from uninvited thoughts that compel them to take action in order to dispel the uncomfortable feelings generated by those thoughts. Their obsessive thoughts are often irrational, like feeling that they will contract a terrible disease from touching doorknobs or other common surfaces, and the actions they are compelled to take are usually highly ritualized, like repetitive hand washing. Even though OCD patients are aware that their fears and concerns are irrational, they find it virtually impossible to resist going through the compulsive rituals that relieve their anxiety. The rituals take a lot of time out of their lives, have adverse effects on their relationships and their sense of self-esteem, and cause a great deal of suffering and disability.

Using PET and fMRI scans, Dr. Schwartz identified specific pathways that carry obsessive thoughts from the thinking brain to the feeling brain. This neural track of synapses, which he calls the "OCD circuit," is identical to the one that earlier UCLA researcher Dr. Lew Baxter called the "worry circuit."

In simple terms, there is an area in our prefrontal cortex

(behind the forehead) that signals when something seems dangerously wrong or isn't what we expected. Messages about this disparity are sent back to a brain region called the striatum (or caudate-putamen complex), which sits right between the cortical thinking brain and the limbic emotional brain. This brain area receives input from both thinking and feeling areas of the brain and then sends signals that either stimulate or suppress a change in our thinking and/or trigger a physical action. In most normal people the situation is resolved fairly quickly by one of these two responses: either we realize that the issue isn't really a problem or we take an action to deal with it. Then we move on to whatever comes next.

In people with OCD, however, and most likely in habitual worriers, the error alarm circuit is stuck in the on position. The uncomfortable feeling of anxiety that results can stimulate obsessive or ruminative worry, or compulsive behaviors such as overeating, excessive drinking, smoking, shopping, or any other action that temporarily relieves the discomfort.

The brilliance of Schwartz's work is that he noticed the immense distress that OCD patients experience from knowing that their thoughts and actions are irrational even while they felt compelled to repeat their ritualistic actions. He reasoned that since these patients were aware of their thoughts and actions, there had to be unaffected areas of the brain that they might be able to use to change their minds and behaviors, and eventually perhaps the malfunctioning parts of their brains.

Schwartz taught a group of OCD patients to increase their ability to observe their obsessive thoughts and develop new ways of responding to them. Explaining the brain circuitry of OCD, he taught his patients to understand that their problem was due to aberrant brain activity rather than to personal weakness or craziness, and to relabel it as such. He trained them to wait fifteen seconds or more before taking any action, and then to refocus their minds on a healthier thought or action to take the place of their typical compulsive behavior.

After ten weeks of group meetings focusing on understanding the nature of OCD and practicing these skills, Schwartz obtained new brain scans on his subjects. He found that the patterns of brain activation were much closer to normal in more than half of them. Their hyperactive worry circuits had been significantly calmed and their brain activity was more balanced. Their symptoms were also greatly relieved—much more so than is typically seen with traditional treatments for OCD.

Schwartz also found that as his OCD patients practiced these new thinking skills, they actually developed a new circuit between the thinking brain and the emotional switching station that inhibits and to some degree overrides the worry circuit. He calls the new pathway the "therapy circuit." Maybe we could call it the "don't worry, be happy" circuit.

Schwartz had demonstrated, for the first time, not only that the mind can change through education, learning, and choice but that it can change the brain when it does. This self-directed neuroplasticity is one of the most important capabilities we have as humans, and Schwartz's demonstration is strong evidence that we can indeed change our worry habits. While changing any well-established thought pattern requires work, habitual worry should be easier to change than the truly driven thinking of Schwartz's OCD patients.

So yes, we can use our minds to change our brains. We can make choices about where we will focus our attention, and those choices can alter long-standing habits and the brain pathways that underlie them. The brain is much more plastic than we previously thought, and it is capable of learning and adapting at virtually any age. Old dogs really *can* learn new tricks.

If the blind can learn to see, you can learn to change your worry habits. If OCD patients can make choices about where to focus their attention, you can, too. Don't let your old brain circuits push you around.

If you've worked through the exercises in the earlier chapters, you've already learned a lot about observing your thoughts, relaxing your mind and body, and thinking in imagery that lets you benefit from the emotional and intuitive intelligence of the silent areas in your brain.

If you skipped directly to this chapter, you can go back now and experiment for yourself with the methods that allow your right brain and limbic brain intelligence to express themselves. Right-brain thinking contains a whole lot of brainpower that will greatly enhance your ability to worry less—and to worry more effectively when you do. In the next chapter we will take a closer look at why right-brain or imagery-based thinking can add so much to your ability to worry well.

9. The Wisdom of Your Emotional/Intuitive Brain

There's a wisdom of the head and . . . a wisdom of the heart.

— CHARLES DICKENS

Our emotional/intuitive brain has formed and guided us since we were born, and maybe even before. It may have begun its work when we first looked into our mother's or father's eyes, felt their touch, breathed in their smell, and heard their voices. Some say that our emotional bonding began even earlier, in the womb, with our responses to our mother's chemistry, heartbeat, and emotions. Once we were born, we reacted to the facial expressions, tone of voice, and body posture of others as well as our own feelings to determine whether we were doing well, were loved and accepted, or were in danger or being threatened. These early perceptions have profound effects on whether we feel that we belong in this world and whether we feel safe.

The effects of emotional bonding have important influences on parents as well. Thomas Lewis, Fari Amini, and Richard Lannon, psychiatrists and authors of *A General Theory of Love*, suggest that the emotional brain evolved in order to protect the young of the species. Reptiles lay many eggs, and even if Mom doesn't take care of them (which she often doesn't), some will survive. Mammals, however, bear live young, and primates like us generally have only one or two babies at a time, so it behooves us to take good care of them. The development of a brain layer that allows bonding, affection, and protective instincts would help make sure that more of our young survive the threats of not only birth but a relatively long period of childhood development. As the emotional part of the brain developed, it became the center of our affiliative impulses, from romantic love and filial devotion to friendships and group dynamics.

As we grow up, our emotional brains continue to be an important influence on how we make friends, interact in social groups, and form crushes or infatuations. Dating, marriage, and children as well as developing and maintaining work relationships and friendships all depend on our fluency and comfort with emotions. As with most abilities, some of us are gifted in this area, some are clueless, and most fall somewhere in between.

While we humans pride ourselves on our intellectual and logical abilities, we are still motivated to a great degree by emotions and instincts that we undervalue and know too little about. We get very little real education in the emotional realm, despite the popularity of the 1995 book *Emotional Intelligence* by *New York Times* science writer Daniel Goleman. Because of our emotional illiteracy, we are plagued by anxiety, depression, violence, and alcohol and drug problems, and we consume too much empty food and too much empty entertainment. I believe that all these symptoms have a lot to do with not knowing how to respond to or cope with strong emotions.

As a physician treating people with chronic illnesses, I cultivated a professional interest in the functioning of the emotional/intuitive brain. A chronic illness's progression depends a great deal on how people care for themselves. For years I thought of care as a behavioral matter, referring to *how* you care for yourself—as in whether you brush your teeth, eat too much junk food, or smoke cigarettes. What I have learned in my forty years of practice is that at its core, self-care really has to do with whether or not you care about yourself in the emotional sense of the word, and thus whether your emotional/intuitive brain is centrally involved.

In my attempts to help my patients, I studied motivational psychology and found that when it came to overall health, the role of feelings was clearly paramount. Most everyone knows about the behaviors that support good health: eating more vegetables, avoiding junk food, exercising regularly, not smoking, managing stress, and trying to lead a meaningful and loving life. It sounds so simple; so why is it so difficult for so many?

I think that self-image is the key—a deep impression woven into the unconscious emotional brain that tells us who we are, what our place is in the world, what we are capable of, and what we deserve. While elements of the self-image are beyond direct awareness, I have found it instructive to ask patients to let an image come to mind that represents their core or essential self. I have been astounded at the variety and emotional power of these images, which have ranged from a "shining star" to a "diamond in the rough" to a "pile of dog crap." You can imagine the differences in life experience that the three people who gave those answers have had, and how these internal perceptions will continue to affect their daily lives.

The feelings that stem from our self-image directly influence how and what we eat, our level of physical activity, what kinds of relationships we seek and develop, and ultimately the state of our health. The grief, disappointment, anger, and fear that can stem from this image or from discrepancies between this image and how we perceive our lives can manifest themselves in many ways. Unresolved emotional pain or conflict often presents itself in the doctor's office, sometimes as anxiety or stress, but often as body pain, fatigue, insomnia, or the toxic effects of coping methods such as smoking, excessive alcohol, poor eating, drug abuse, or type A behavior.

For many years I've listened carefully to my patients in order to understand where their pain and suffering comes from, and also to identify ways that they might be able to resolve or heal themselves. Like most therapeutically oriented people, I learned to listen between the words, for the change in tone of voice or posture or the unintended Freudian slip that might lead me to the emotional core that is the matrix of most physical symptoms. Sometimes I could help a patient identify the source of her suffering, but many times it remained elusive and hard to understand. Then I learned to work with imagery, the native language of the emotional brain, and it became much easier to understand how mind, body, and spirit interacted.

IMAGERY AS THE ROSETTA STONE OF THE EMOTIONAL BRAIN

The Rosetta stone is an ancient piece of basalt discovered in Rosetta, Egypt, in 1799, by the troops of Napoleon Bonaparte. It was found to have the same information carved on it in

three languages: ancient Egyptian hieroglyphics, a more recent Egyptian script, and classical Greek. Because Greek was a
known language, scholars were finally able to decipher the hieroglyphics and unlock secrets that had eluded them for many
centuries.

Martin Horowitz, a professor of psychiatry at the University of California, San Francisco, says that the brain encodes
our experience into three basic forms of mental representa-
tion: the "enactive" or physical, the "lexical" or verbal, and the
image. In trying to understand symptoms of illness, a patient
will usually tell her doctor about them, so both the physical and
verbal aspects of the situation are represented, but how they
are connected usually remains a mystery. Inviting the unconscious emotional/intuitive mind to provide images about the
situation frequently reveals what the body is communicating
through its symptoms. The imagery often allows us to understand the situation more clearly, and leads to addressing emotional patterns that can help resolve the pattern of distress. Let
me give you an example.

Danica, a twenty-eight-year-old assistant bank manager, had
a long-standing problem with her weight. She was particularly
prone to overeating at night. "I know what I should eat, and for
the most part, I eat well," she told me. "Then all of a sudden I'll
find myself staring at the shredded wrapper of a giant choco-
late bar. It's like someone else took over my body!"

I encouraged Danica to let an image come to mind that
represented the part of her that felt compelled to eat that way.
A frenetic honeybee flying in chaotic patterns came to mind.
Danica said it reminded her of the uncomfortable way that she
felt most of the time. I asked her to invite another image that
would help the bee settle down, and a lovely flower came to
mind. She imagined holding the flower out, and as the frantic

bee landed on it and drank its nectar, the bee became more and more content. Danica started to relax at the same time. When I next saw her, she said that she had used this simple image to calm and center herself when she began to feel anxious and scattered. She also found that the bee imagery reminded her to look for things that were enjoyable and satisfying during her day, and not to simply run around trying to satisfy everyone else's expectations. She found that stopping for lunch and snacks, breathing deeply, taking short breaks, and seeing the humor in a situation calmed and energized her the way the flower calmed and energized the bee. She told me, "I see that if I don't get physically and emotionally nourished during the day, I am more likely to pig out sometime later that night." As Danica learned to take better care of herself, she found that her nighttime cravings quickly diminished and eventually went away.

IMAGERY IS AN OLD AND VERY NATURAL FORM OF THINKING

Imagination is older than rational thinking, and it helped our ancestors survive for millions of years before language appeared on the scene. As animals developed the ability to move, they needed a way to take some kind of map of their environment along with them, or else they'd never make it back to the web, or den, or wherever they lived. A tiger roaming his territory must have some kind of internal map of the area, in which his prey, their hiding places, water, and potential dangers are all represented. A house cat running downstairs when she hears the electric can opener must have a map in her brain that helps her navigate the shortest path to her dinner.

At some unknown time in prehistory, the human brain's ability to map its environment in space developed into an ability to imagine its environment in time and to imagine a different environment. That evolutionary change is the mother of both creativity and our ability to worry, because things are frequently not the way we would prefer them to be. This discrepancy between the real and the imagined is the root of suffering.

In human history, pictures of human experience existed long before written descriptions. Drawings on cave walls in southern France predate the first written languages by at least fifteen thousand years. They testify to a well-developed visual appreciation of animals and events in our prehistory, and to our ancestors' ability to graphically represent their surroundings and experiences.

When we look at the earliest written languages, they tend to be pictorial, with pictures representing objects, and then gradually evolving to represent more abstract concepts. Egyptian hieroglyphics and Chinese ideograms are good examples of these pictorial languages.

The way intelligence develops in childhood also shows us that imagery is an older, more "time-tested" way of thinking than words. As infants, we begin to imagine and fantasize at an early age, constructing an inner world that is populated with the faces and voices of our parents, siblings, relatives, friends, and pets, along with the sights, sounds, and tactile sensations of other elements of our new world. We learn to color and draw before we learn to read and write, and we spend a great deal of time in our inner worlds as we try to integrate the enormous amount of data we take in every day. Later, as we are taught to read, write, and do arithmetic, our brains change, and more of our attention goes to learning the logical thinking that will serve us well as adults.

Unfortunately, once this type of left-brain education begins, few of us ever get taught how to use our imaginations skillfully to foster creativity, problem solving, and emotional intelligence. Our right-brain intelligence is often neglected and even discouraged in favor of rational thinking. This is a mistake with many adverse consequences.

In their book *Passion and Reason: Making Sense of Our Emotions*, psychologists Richard Lazarus and Bernice Lazarus write, "Emotions are a vital tool for getting along in the world. They evolved as they have in our species because they aid us in making our way successfully through life." They also point out that "emotions and intelligence go hand in hand, which is why humans, highly intelligent beings, are such emotional animals."

That is why it is important for us to become more literate in imagery. It is the native language of our emotional/intuitive brains. Just as the Rosetta stone helped us to decipher hieroglyphics, imagery can help us better understand the emotional, intuitive wisdom often hidden in our worries, health behaviors, and physical symptoms.

OLDER DOESN'T MEAN BETTER

Just because it's an evolutionarily older way of thinking doesn't necessarily make imagery a better way to think, but it does represent a much longer experience of dealing with human life issues, especially those having to do with relationships and emotions. Learning to use the natural language of the emotional brain can help us avoid or reduce much of the worry, anxiety, and stress that these issues can stir up.

Imagery is the language of dreams and daydreams, memories and reminiscences, plans, projections, and possibilities. It is the language of the arts, the emotions, your deeper self, and the brain regions in which that ancient wisdom abides. It is the neurological royal road to reconnecting with the deep emotional and intuitive wisdom that has guided us to thrive, or at least survive, for hundreds of millions of years. When we aren't sure what to do, or when we have a problem that we can't figure out, imagery makes room for the silent, emotional, intuitive areas of our brains to express themselves and add their wisdom to our perspective.

Julie, a forty-six-year-old health professional, volunteered to be a demonstration subject in an imagery class I was teaching. She told me that she had been suffering severe pain in both forearms for over three years. It had been diagnosed as a form of tendonitis and she had seen many doctors for it. Nothing had helped her, including intensive physical therapy, splints, and even sizable doses of narcotic medications.

I led Julie through a relaxation process and then invited her to let an image come to mind that could tell her something useful about the pain. Black steel rods in her arms came quickly to mind. She didn't understand what they had to do with her pain, so I asked her what qualities she noticed in the rods, and she said they were rigid, cold, and unyielding. She than added that as she had been telling me about these qualities, an image of her grandfather suddenly arose. I asked her to just observe it and see what thoughts came with the image. She said that she had cared for her grandfather in his last two years of his life, because she was his only remaining relative. Julie said that her grandfather was a difficult person and noticed that he had the same qualities that the image conveyed. He was hard, cold, and unyielding, and that had made it especially hard to care for him. She also recalled that she had developed her arm pain during the time she spent with him.

I invited Julie to imagine that she could talk with the image of her grandfather. She said she wanted to ask him why he was the way he was, something she had never dared to ask him in real life. When she did that, I encouraged her to imagine that he could communicate back to her in a way she could understand. In her imagination, her grandfather said that he had been brought up to be the way he was, and he was very sorry that he hadn't been able to express his softer emotions to her. He said that he loved her very much and appreciated all the help and love that she had given him. She felt a sense of warmth from him and was both surprised and deeply moved. After a while I suggested that she thank him for coming, and she imagined that he reached out and hugged her.

Julie felt very relieved after this imagery session. We reviewed her experience for a few minutes, and then I asked her to notice how her arms felt. She was surprised to find that her pain level was quite a bit lower than when she started.

Afterward, Julie went to a grief counselor who supported her in continuing to "talk" to her grandfather this way. Her pain completely resolved after about six sessions and didn't return.

One of the many interesting things about Julie's story is that the imagery led her to an awareness of the connection between her feelings and her physical pain, a connection that we know is there but often have trouble understanding from a rational perspective. The imagery added the missing information that had made it difficult for Julie and her doctors to understand why her arms hurt so much for so long.

Imagery seems able to take us for a virtual glass-bottomed boat ride into our unconscious minds and to let information come to light from that hidden source of intelligence. We might say that Julie's non-verbal, emotional brain was crying out through her body, until she learned how to let it express itself more directly. Once she heard, felt, and understood its message, her emotional brain was able to stop signaling for attention.

A Few Other Advantages of
Imagery-Based Thinking

Besides its close connection to emotion, imagery is an unusually efficient way for your brain to code, store, access, and process complex information. For example, recall an experience you've had that made you feel very happy, and that you'd be happy to remember now. Imagine for a few moments that you are there again. Notice what you see, hear, and feel there.

If I now asked you to write or tell me about that experience, I bet that you could write several sentences, perhaps even several pages, and that it might take you from a few minutes to half an hour. But I also bet that the memories of the sights, sounds, and smells came back much more quickly than that, and brought the good feelings of the experience back with them. The images are a rapid-access conduit to the multidimensional memory, which includes not only the sensory details but also your feelings at the time. In fact, it is the strong feelings accompanying any event that tell the brain that a memory is worth storing for the long term.

Another important aspect of imagery-based thinking is that it is a potent stimulator of physiology. If you think about salivating, for instance, you might produce a few drops, but if you vividly imagine sucking on a lemon, you will probably salivate much more. Or consider the effects of sexual fantasy if you want to understand how powerfully imagining something can affect your body and mind. As you already learned, you can stimulate either a stress response or a relaxation response, depending on the thoughts and images you choose to focus on.

Finally, because imagery is the brain language that lets us use simultaneous information processing, it can quickly show us the big picture of a situation and many, if not all, of its interconnected threads. It complements the sequential information processing type of thinking we do with words and numbers, which lets us analyze situations and break them down into their separate components. Julie's case is a good example of how imagery helps us see the forest as well as the individual trees.

Psychologist Robert Ornstein uses a metaphor to help us understand the differences between these two ways of thinking. Imagine two observers watching a train traveling along a track. One observer, analogous to the logical left brain with its sequential-processing type of thinking, is at trackside, and his perception of the train is that one car passes by at a time, followed by the others, one after the other. The second observer, analogous to the synthetic, simultaneous, right-brain type of thinking, is in a hot-air balloon several hundred feet above the track. From this position she can see the whole train, the countryside it is traveling through, the town it left and the town it is going to, and the sunrise coming up over the mountain in the distance. She instantaneously sees what the whole train looks like as well as the lay of the land through which it travels, and sees how they are all related.

Again, one type of thinking is not better than the other, but each has its strengths in different arenas. Rational, sequential thinking lets us plan, quantify, invent, build, and make time-bound agreements. Synthetic, simultaneous thinking lets us appreciate and understand where we are in relation to the people, places, and possibilities that surround us. Each form of

thinking is appropriate in different situations. Trying to emotionally balance your checkbook and arguing logically with an
upset teenager are examples of applying the wrong type of intelligence to two very different situations.

How Is Intuition Connected to Emotions?

As we think about the emotional nature of the unconscious
mind, and understand that much of that is connected to both
right-brain and limbic-brain processing, we also must consider
the way emotions are connected to intuition. Intuition is the
art of knowing without the use of reason or logic. The word
stems from a Latin root that means "to look inside." Paying attention to the expressions of our inner world allows us to sense
and use internal guidance as we navigate our life journeys,
drawing from both the emotional and instinctive wisdoms that
live there.

Intuition is closely related to vigilance as well as emotion.
In fact, it is so intertwined with vigilance and fear that differen-
tiating them is critical to using intuition effectively. Dr. Judith
Orloff, author of *Second Sight* and *Emotional Freedom*, says that
true intuition is characterized by a feeling of "rightness" in the
gut, an unemotional delivery of information, and a compassionate, affirming tone. This is the modus operandi of an inner
wisdom figure, a messenger symbol that often makes intuition
more accessible.

Fear, on the other hand, is highly emotional, sometimes
panicky, and doesn't come from a quiet, centered place. This
doesn't mean that fear isn't worth listening to when there's a
rustling in the bush; it's just different from intuitive intelli-

gence. Intuition draws on the silent, unconscious perceptions of the areas of the brain that pay attention to emotional expression and big-picture connections. Intuition is a function of the preverbal brain that helped all of our ancestors survive the many challenges to their existence and which draws its wisdom from a huge range of life experience.

SCIENCE PROGRESSES THROUGH INTUITION AS MUCH AS REASON

Intuition is crucial not only to personal relationships and circumstances but to the advancement of human knowledge through science as well—a truth acknowledged by our greatest scientists. Albert Einstein once said, "The only real valuable thing is intuition," and also claimed that "imagination is more important than knowledge." Dr. Jonas Salk, discoverer of the polio vaccine, agreed, saying, "Intuition will tell the thinking mind where to look next."

Both of these eminent thinkers were aware of the role of intuition in scientific breakthroughs. Einstein said that his theory of relativity came to him while he was listening to music. In fact, when he was stumped by a physics problem, he often listened to music while letting his mind drift, finding that solutions that had evaded his rational analysis would often come to him in that relaxed state.

August Kekulé was one of the most prominent professors of chemistry in nineteenth-century Europe. He and his colleagues struggled for years to understand the chemical structure of benzene, since the scientific knowledge of the time could not account for all of its properties. As the story goes, Kekulé drifted into a daydream and saw the image of a snake holding its own tail in its mouth. He recognized at once that the benzene molecule was a circular chain of carbon atoms. This discovery was a crucial key to understanding the chemistry of living organisms and the beginning of the science of organic chemistry. In science, as in daily life, intellect and intuition are complementary strategies for understanding our world and for solving its challenges.

While we all learned the logical languages of reading, writing, and arithmetic in school, most of us have never had any formal education in how to use the emotional language of imagery. That's one reason why it is so powerful when you reclaim it, and why I have taken such pains to teach you some fundamentally important ways to use it. If you have worked through the exercises in *The Worry Solution*, you have learned that imagery can help you relax, expand your mental and emotional capabilities, and draw on deeper levels of wisdom and creativity. Imagery lets you bring all your brainpower to bear on dealing with difficult life issues and managing stress, anxiety, and worry.

Because the imagination is the source of most worry, it stands to reason that it would be a potent tool for reducing or eliminating worry as well. Imagery-based thinking is holistic and synthetic, giving us big-picture information. It offers us a chance to see how emotions and the body are related, as it did with Julie's arm pain. Imagery has a close connection to creativity and problem solving because it lets us see old situations from new perspectives and draws on an ancient well of experience. Imagery-based thinking also turbo-boosts your ability to shift emotional states as you choose, and strengthen the qualities that you most value in yourself. This may be the most liberating aspect of all, and I will teach you how to do this in the next chapter.

Ultimately, the goal is not to be a left-brain or right-brain thinker but to be a whole-brain thinker, able not only to logically analyze a situation but to relate to it emotionally and intuitively as well. We want to be able to use whichever of our mental functions is most appropriate for solving our problems, resolving our worries, and letting us live with the greatest amount of both freedom and happiness. These two ways of thinking are our birthrights. We just need to claim them and learn to use them both well.

10. Strengthening Your Best Qualities

✳

Imagination is a good horse to carry you over the ground, not a magic carpet to take you away from the world of possibilities.

— ROBERTSON DAVIES

✳

If you've worked through the practices in this book so far, you've learned to relax, to observe your own thoughts and feelings, to sort out your worries, to transform those you cannot do anything about, and to take effective action when there is something you can do. You've also learned how to connect to a deeper source of wisdom within you when things aren't clear or you need extra help.

Now I want to teach you an imagery meditation that focuses on strengthening personal qualities that can help you shift moods at will, build your inner strengths, and make difficult situations easier to surmount. You can use this Best Quality imagery anytime you feel that you need more of some particular quality in order to move forward, accept, let go, forgive, or change something in your life.

Janelle, thirty-four, came to see me after her boyfriend of six years left her. Sobbing uncontrollably, Janelle told me over and over again, barely able to get the words out, that she didn't think she could live through the pain. I asked her what quality she felt she needed more of, and she said, "I need more strength—I don't think I can make it through this without more strength, and maybe more faith, too."

I invited her to go back in her imagination to a time when she felt that she'd had that kind of strength and faith inside. She recalled the death of a beloved uncle ten years earlier. While she had been bereft, she remembered having felt a type of strength and a sense of faith that allowed her to provide emotional support to her aunt. I urged Janelle to imagine that she was back there again and to notice what she'd seen, heard, smelled, and felt at the time. As she did that, I asked her to notice where she felt the sensations of strength and faith in her body. We took some time to let those feelings grow larger and stronger until she felt as if every cell were touched and filled with strength and faith. Soon her face grew calm and she unconsciously sat up straighter. After several minutes, I invited her to come back to the present, bringing the feelings of strength and faith back with her. When she opened her eyes, she looked at me and said, "You know, I *do* have the strength I need, but I just couldn't get to it."

Of course, Janelle still had a lot of grief and some difficult emotional challenges to face, but now she was reconnected with her strength and her faith, and had a way to connect with them again if she got frightened and lost touch. I saw her again after a week and she told me, "I am using that technique almost daily and feel myself getting stronger and having more faith in myself every time."

What Is a Personal Quality?

A personal quality is a characteristic that helps make up your personality. Qualities are not emotions, but people with certain qualities tend to express particular emotions more often, and also tend to evoke certain emotions in others. A person who is carefree and kind often expresses joy and empathy and tends to evoke feelings of affection and calmness in others, whereas a person who is gruff and aggressive will more likely express anger and annoyance and evoke wariness, fear, or anger in others.

Personal qualities can either attract or repel people, and can make a difference in whether a person is successful in work, relationships, or life in general. Employers tend to value people who are punctual, easy to get along with, conscientious, and responsible, while friends may appreciate spontaneity, loyalty, and a sense of humor. Few people will like arrogance, selfishness, or rudeness.

Most of us are capable of displaying different qualities in different situations. The Best Quality meditation helps you strengthen the qualities you'd like to have more of in a particular situation—especially in circumstances that have you feeling anxious or worried. It's another kind of positive worry, but instead of focusing on the outcome you want, you focus on the way you'd most like to be. Best Quality imagery can help you act with more confidence and creativity and boost the like-lihood of your success much more than if you unconsciously "prepare" by worrying about how frightened, self-conscious, or stupid you might appear to be.

Here's a partial list of some personal qualities that people generally value and that may help you be more successful in reaching your goals. It's not a comprehensive list. I've left out qualities such as grumpiness, irritability, offensiveness, or flatu-lence, for instance, which rarely help anyone get ahead; nor will you find such qualities as aggressiveness, dominance, or ruthlessness, which may well help you survive if you are in com-bat or play professional football but are not generally welcome in polite company.

The qualities listed below are ones that most often help people in common yet important social, work, and family situ-ations. If a quality you could use more of is missing from the list, name it and use that as your focus in your Best Quality meditation. The purpose of this process is to help you experi-ence more of whatever qualities will be most useful to you.

First, just read through the qualities listed below. Which qualities do you identify in yourself? Which ten qualities do you feel best describe you, regardless of whether they are on the list? What qualities, if any, would you like to experience or express more strongly or frequently?

accepting	accommodating	accurate	adaptable
adventurous	ambitious	analytical	appreciative
approachable	articulate	assertive	authentic
autonomous	calm	candid	cautious
cheerful	collaborative	committed	compassionate
competitive	confident	congenial	conscientious
conservative	considerate	consistent	cooperative

cost-conscious	creative	curious	decisive
dedicated	dependable	detail-oriented	determined
diplomatic	disciplined	discreet	driven
dynamic	eager	efficient	empathetic
energetic	enjoyable	enthusiastic	entrepreneurial
ethical	fair	flexible	forgiving
friendly	generous	goal-oriented	hardworking
helpful	honest	humorous	imaginative
inclusive	independent	industrious	influential
innovative	inquisitive	intelligent	intuitive
kind	level-headed	loyal	mature
methodical	observant	open-minded	optimistic
organized	outgoing	passionate	patient
perceptive	persistent	personable	persuasive
pleasant	poised	polite	practical
precise	process-oriented	productive	professional
punctual	rational	realistic	reasonable
reliable	resilient	resourceful	respectful
responsible	responsive	results-oriented	self-aware
self-motivated	self-reliant	self-sufficient	sincere
spontaneous	tactful	team-oriented	tenacious
thorough	thoughtful	tolerant	trustworthy
values-oriented	versatile	vigorous	visionary

How Might You Use Best Quality Imagery?

Best Quality imagery can help you in many ways in your efforts to worry well. You can use it to help you accept or transform worries or to develop qualities that will enable you to take effective action. But you can also use this technique anytime you feel lacking in something—anytime you think you don't have enough courage, patience, strength, perseverance, resilience, or any other quality that would help you cope better. You can use a Best Quality meditation to build motivation and confidence as you contemplate an action plan you've devised, and you can use it to evoke qualities that you want to take into a job interview, an important meeting, or an athletic, speaking, or artistic performance. You can also use a Best Quality meditation to prepare yourself before having important talks with your family members or your boss, or before you go on a date.

Best Quality imagery is also a great way to start your day, whether you are aiming to cultivate more patience with your kids or develop more confidence at work. It can help set you up for the day by getting you to focus on how you prefer to be, instead of how you don't want to be. It's similar to Positive Worry imagery, but with an extra emphasis on amplifying a felt sense of the qualities you would like to cultivate more of.

In Best Quality imagery you use the sensory details of a memory or image to remind you how it feels to have the qualities you want. Recalling a time when you felt and expressed these qualities, you can draw on what that experience looked like, sounded like in your voice, and—most important—felt like in your body and your face. You'll then use your imagination to amplify these feelings and bring them into the present, so you can embody the qualities you want as you carry them into your day.

You've already used Best Quality imagery a couple of times in earlier imagery exercises we've done—to enhance your sense of relaxation, calmness, and peacefulness—and again at the end of the imagery rehearsal piece you did as part of your Effective Action process. It was the part where you noticed how it felt to have been successful, either in relaxing or in attaining your goal, and then let that feeling grow bigger and stronger until it filled your whole body. By paying special attention to your body posture and your face as you experience the qualities you want to enhance, you tune in to two of the most important nonverbal indicators of how you feel, which in turn lets you experience the qualities more strongly.

Research has shown that much of our emotional state is conveyed through body language and facial expression, and that in most people the right hemisphere of the brain is specially equipped to both notice and communicate these emotional cues. When pictures of facial expressions are shown only to our left hemisphere, we cannot distinguish happy from sad, or fearful from angry; our right hemisphere, on the other hand, is extremely accurate and sensitive to the slightest indications of these emotional states.

Dr. Paul Ekman, emeritus professor of psychology at the University of California, San Francisco, has studied facial expression of emotions for decades. He has found that humans, whether jungle-dwelling hunters in Borneo or housewives in Queens, express specific emotions with identical facial expressions. The things that make people feel happy, sad, angry, or fearful may differ by culture, but when people experience a certain emotion, they express it with the same movements of their facial muscles.

Once Ekman identified the facial muscle patterns that denoted specific emotions, he used biofeedback equipment to train college students to mimic these facial patterns by simply replicating the muscle movement involved. He'd instruct the students to "relax the orbicularis oris" or "contract the corrugator muscle" until their faces were mimicking the expression of joy, fear, or anger. When they arranged their faces this way, the students accurately reported that they felt the emotion they were portraying, even though no emotion had been named and no emotional prompts were given to them.

That's why we pay so much attention to imagining body posture, facial expression, and tone of voice when using Best Quality imagery. Mentally attending to these cues will stimulate the feeling of that emotion or quality in you, allowing you to amplify it and take it with you into situations where it will be useful.

USING BEST QUALITY IMAGERY IN SPECIFIC SITUATIONS

Now let's apply Best Quality imagery to a specific situation that may be worrying you. This could be a situation that you want to let go of, accept, or act on and change. If you want to release or accept the situation, the qualities you might want to focus on include acceptance, realism, compassion, and resilience. If it's a situation you want to change, you might benefit more from courage, confidence, creativity, or perseverance.

As you contemplate the situation, ask yourself what qualities would help you carry out your chosen action. Remember that both accepting and letting go are actions, even if they are internal.

I find that the Best Quality meditation works best when you focus on no more than three qualities at one time. More than that muddies the waters and makes it difficult to feel any particular quality. It also makes it less likely that you'll have memories of a time when you experienced that particular combination of qualities.

As always, you want to go into your inner world with a

purpose—in this case to access and strengthen particular qualities. Let yourself start with one to three qualities, and hold them softly because as you shift your attention to your inner world, your unconscious mind may offer up other qualities that turn out to be even more helpful.

Leslie needed to talk to her husband, Tom, about his increasing irritability and alcohol consumption. She knew he had been under a great deal of stress at work that was compounded by increasing concerns about money. Their kids were getting close to college age and Tom's long-standing habit of using credit cards when he lacked the cash to pay for something was threatening to overwhelm them financially. Leslie had tried to discuss her concerns with Tom several times only to be ignored or rudely rebuffed. She felt that she no longer knew how to reach her husband. She knew she had to address her worries with him somehow, and as she thought about how to approach him, she decided she needed to have more courage and assertiveness so that she could insist that he talk to her about these issues.

As Leslie relaxed and went to her inner world to strengthen these qualities, she was surprised by a different image that quickly came to mind. It was a memory of her and Tom on their honeymoon, relaxing in front of a fire after making love. She recalled how close she had felt to Tom, and how safe. She was saddened to realize that was no longer the case, and she sensed that Tom felt very alone, too. A sense of compassion for him began to stir alongside her fear and irritation. While she knew she had to act, it began to dawn on her that taking a demanding stance was unlikely to bring the results she wanted.

Instead, she found herself imagining being with Tom again in a relaxed, intimate way and telling him how much she loved him and that she was aware that things were hard for him. She also imagined telling him that she would always be his partner, and that he needed to confide in her and trust that they could work things out together. In her imagination he became tearful and admitted that he was reluctant to share things with her because he felt he was letting her and their children down. He was terrified and ashamed at the idea of not being able to properly provide for his family. He hated to seem weak or out of control, even though that was very much how he felt.

In her imagery, Leslie reassured Tom that she didn't see him as weak but was concerned that he could let them all down if he retreated into alcohol and isolation. She let him know that she needed him to stay strong and that he could trust her to stay strong, too. In her mind's eye he seemed relieved, and she imagined them embracing each other.

Leslie came back from this imagery with a desire to reconnect to Tom by showing him more love. She told Tom she had a surprise for him. After taking the kids to her parents' house for a weekend, she cooked a special meal and uncorked a good bottle of wine. They didn't have a fireplace, so she put a DVD of a burning Yule log on the TV. After dinner she told him that she loved him and was concerned about them feeling so distant. She told him about her memories of their early love and her desire to rekindle those feelings. They cuddled for some time on the couch, which eventually led to a sweet lovemaking session. They fell asleep in each other's arms, and when they woke up in the middle of the night they made love again, for the first time in a long time. Afterward Tom started sharing his concerns with her, as did she with him, and they agreed that if they worked as a team, they could handle whatever challenges came along. Tom promised to stop drinking for a while, and he did. They saw a financial counselor and worked on a budget together, and both felt much less anxious, worried, and alone than they had before.

Leslie's rational assessment of the situation led her to conclude that she needed to take the bull by the horns—and indeed, that might have been necessary if things hadn't worked out so well. But Leslie's emotional, relational brain knew much better how to relate to Tom in his distress. If Leslie had been abused, disrespected, or taken advantage of for a long time, she well may have needed to assert herself to restore the relationship, or to consider a separation if that approach failed. In this case, however, she was simply part of a couple in distress, with a husband who had one wheel coming off and was trying to cope in an unhealthy and ineffective manner. Her love, warmth, kindness, and empathy allowed her to reconnect with Tom so they could work on their issues together.

Leslie's goal was to help her husband get out of a downward spiral, protecting him, their children, and their future along the way. If the situation were different, if Tom had become a chronic drunk, abdicating his responsibilities, emotionally or physical abusing her or the children, another action might have been required—one involving courage, assertiveness, and probably confrontation. Here, a dose of patience, love, and understanding paid off much better. Leslie's emotional brain understood that, and when she was quiet and went inside herself, her imagery guided her to a successful resolution of the problem.

Leslie's story is another good example of how the use of imagery can improve both top-down and bottom-up communication between the thinking and emotional brains. In some situations your thinking, conscious brain may know that there are better qualities than fear to bring into the situation, and it will lead the emotional brain to memories that provide access to those qualities. In other situations, your emotional brain can show you the most effective remedy because it has been there observing with its big-picture perspective all along, registering relevant data about you, your spouse, your family, and other relationships. It's hardly surprising that your own brain is better than any how-to book at bringing forth ideas custom-tailored to your situation. Using imagery to invite this ancient source of emotional and intuitive wisdom into your deliberations gives you the best chance of responding effectively and humanely to almost any situation you encounter.

Your Turn

Now it's your turn to experiment with the Best Quality imagery process. Like all the techniques in this book, this one is most effective when you first take the time to relax and bring your focus inside, letting most of the outside distractions in your life slip away. The relaxation and deep inner focus allow this imagery to become "front-page news" for your brain and make a deeper impression than if it's simply one of the thousands of thoughts you have as the day goes by.

If you are preparing for an important action or change in behavior and you have enough time in advance, practice this method for several weeks, using it once or even twice a day. After some practice it will become second nature to you, and when it does, you will find yourself able to quickly recall images that let you feel the qualities you need in whatever situation you find yourself.

As with any acquired skill, the more you practice, the easier and more natural it becomes. If you have something coming up soon, however, doing this exercise even once can help you connect to the qualities you want to strengthen.

PREPARING FOR BEST QUALITY IMAGERY

As usual, get yourself comfortable and see to it that you won't be disturbed for about twenty or thirty minutes unless there is a true emergency. Take a few moments and think about your situation and the qualities you need more of. Read the meditation script or have it read to you, or listen to the audio of me guiding you through it, which you can get at www.worrysolution.com.

BEST QUALITY IMAGERY

Let yourself begin to relax in the usual way. Let your breathing get a little deeper and fuller, but still comfortable, and with every breath in, notice that you bring in fresh air, fresh oxygen, fresh energy that fuels your body. And with every breath out, imagine that you can release a little bit of tension, a bit of discomfort, or a bit of worry...

And let that deeper breathing and your thoughts of fresh energy in and tension and worry out be an invitation to your body and mind to begin to relax, to begin to shift gears, and just let it be an easy and natural movement, without having to force anything, without having to make anything happen right now. Just letting it happen, breathing and relaxing, breathing and energizing...

Let yourself come back to taking a few deeper breaths whenever you feel the need to relax even more deeply, but for now, let your breathing take its own natural rate and its own natural rhythm, and simply let the gentle movement of your body as it breathes

---

allow you to relax naturally and comfortably, almost without having to try ...

And to relax more deeply, simply notice how your right foot feels right now, and notice how your left foot feels. And noticing that just before you probably weren't aware of your feet at all, but now that you turn your attention to them, you can notice them and how they feel ...

And notice what happens when you silently invite your feet to relax, to become soft and at ease, and allow them to relax in their own way, without worrying about how deeply or easily they relax. And in the same way, invite your legs to relax, and let the intelligence in your legs respond as your legs become more comfortable and at ease ...

And simply notice any release or relaxation that happens without having to make any effort at all, without worrying about how you relax or how deeply you relax, just allowing the legs to soften and release, and letting it be a comfortable and very pleasant experience ...

And you can relax even more deeply and comfortably if you want to by continuing to notice different parts of your body and simply inviting them to soften and relax, and allowing them to relax in their own way. And you only relax as deeply as is comfortable for you, and if you ever need to return your awareness to the outer world, you can do that by simply opening your eyes and looking around and coming fully alert. And if you need to respond to anything there, you can do that, and knowing that you can do that if you need to, you can relax again and return your attention to the inner world of your imagination ...

Inviting your low back, pelvis, hips, and genital area to release and relax, and your abdomen and midsection, softening and releasing. And your chest and rib cage relaxing as well, without effort or struggle, just letting go and staying aware as you do ...

Inviting your back and spine to soften and release, across your low back, midback, between and across your shoulder blades, and across your neck and shoulders, and addressing your arms and elbows and forearms, and inviting those areas of your body to soften and relax, and go to a more comfortable state of being. Inviting your wrists to relax, your hands, and the palms of your hands, your fingers and your thumbs...

Noticing your face and jaw muscles, and inviting them to relax as well, to become soft and at ease. Inviting your scalp and forehead to become soft and at ease, and your eyes, and even your tongue can be relaxed...

And as you relax comfortably, let your attention shift from your outer world to your inner world, the world inside that only you can see, hear, smell, and feel. The world where your memories, your dreams, your feelings, and your plans all reside. A world that you can learn to connect with, and that can help you in many ways on your journey...

And to go deeper, imagine that you go inside to a very special place, a very beautiful place where you feel comfortable and relaxed, yet very aware. This may be a place that you've actually visited at some time in your life, in the outer world or in the inner world. It may be a place that you've seen somewhere, or it may be a new place that you haven't visited before, and none of that matters, as long as it's a very beautiful place to you, a place that's inviting and that feels very good to be in, a place that feels safe and secure to you...

If there's more than one place that comes to mind, pick the one that attracts you the most right now and begin to explore it. And notice what you imagine seeing there...all the things and objects you see, the colors, the shapes. Don't worry at all about how you imagine this place, as long as it's beautiful to you, and feels safe and secure...

Notice if there are any sounds you imagine hearing in this place, or if it's simply very quiet. Notice if there's a fragrance or aroma that you imagine there, or perhaps a special quality of the air. There may or may not be, and it's perfectly all right, however you imagine this place of deep relaxation and comfort. And it may change over time as you explore it, or it may stay the same. It doesn't really matter. Just let yourself explore a little more, and imagine that you're there right now.

What time of day does it seem to be there, and what time of year, and what's the temperature like? Take some time to find a spot where you feel safe and comfortable, and let yourself get situated there…And just notice how it feels to imagine yourself there right now, and let it be a comfortable experience. And if your mind wanders from time to time, take another deep breath or two and gently return your attention to this beautiful and healing place just for now, without feeling the need to go anywhere else right now, without needing to do anything else, just for now…

And now think about the quality or qualities that you'd like to feel more of in yourself. Silently name them, or say them aloud if you wish, and let your mind take you to a time when you felt these qualities in yourself, and imagine that you're there once again. And notice where you are, and notice what you're doing, if anything, and who you are with, if anyone.

Take some time to notice the details. Notice what you see as you look around, and notice what you hear. Let yourself be there now in your own way. Notice if there are any smells or aromas, and how it feels to be there. And if there was never a time when you felt these qualities in yourself, you might bring to mind someone else that you've noticed these qualities in, perhaps someone you know, or even a historical or imaginary figure … …

Or you might simply imagine what it would feel like if you did feel these qualities in you more strongly…

And then imagine that those qualities are in you now…and pay special attention to the feelings of the qualities you came to experience...Notice how it feels to have them within you, and notice where you feel them most strongly in your body. Gently scan with your attention through your body, and notice if these feelings seem to center anywhere, if they're stronger in one area than another, in your face or head, in your chest, your abdomen, pelvis...arms or legs, anywhere else...

And as you feel these qualities that you desire to cultivate, notice how your body posture is as you feel those qualities within you... and notice how your face feels as you allow the feelings of those qualities to be there...and how do you imagine your voice sounds and feels as you talk while being in touch with these qualities within you?...And how do you imagine that you move, as you sense these qualities in you?

If you're comfortable with it, imagine that you can allow the sense of these qualities to grow a bit stronger within you, to gently grow and expand...Simply stay relaxed and comfortable, and imagine that the feelings begin to grow so that they fill your whole body...as if every cell of your body were touched by these qualities and the feelings that go with these qualities you desire...

Take some time to let the feelings develop...just like a photograph develops...Imagine that the feelings from these qualities radiate out from wherever they are centered, radiating out in all directions, like the light from the sun, imagining that it fills your body with this quality or qualities...imagining that you feel it all the way down your legs to the bottoms of your feet...and all the way down your arms to the palms of your hands...and the tips of your fingers and thumbs... and feeling your face...and touching the very deepest core of your being...and all your organs and your bones and your muscles...

And all the other tissues and cells in your body...imagine that they soak up these qualities like a sponge...allowing yourself to become saturated with them...naming them again silently or out loud...

Then if you like, imagine that you have a knob or control, as you do on a radio or television, and you can turn up the strength of the qualities, just like you'd turn up the volume on a radio...And imagine turning up the volume so that the feelings of the qualities overflow your body so they fill a space around your body for a foot in every direction...and notice how that feels...

And if you like, you can turn it up even stronger, so you can imagine filling the space around you for several feet in every direction... and stronger yet to fill the room around you...with those qualities you desire...You can imagine turning the strength of the feelings up as much as you like...to fill the town you're in...or the whole world, if you like...just imagine turning it up as far as you like, and don't turn it up any more if you feel at all uncomfortable at any point... And you can turn it back down to where it feels comfortable to you at any time...

Bigger isn't necessarily better. Just adjust the feeling to whatever is most pleasant to you right now...It's like listening to a radio when you're the only one in a room...Whatever is most comfortable to you right now is exactly right...There is no right or wrong strength to feel this at, so let yourself adjust the strength of the feeling to be most comfortable for you now...and simply notice where that is... and enjoy that for a few minutes more...and feel free at any time to adjust it either way...

And you can let those feelings stay with you as long as you like, and even bring them back with you when you decide to return your attention to the outer world...and taking all the time you need..........

And now, when you are ready to return your attention to the outer world...silently express any appreciation you might have for having a special place of relaxation and safety within you...a place you can come to for deep relaxation, renewal, and to make changes in the way you think and feel...and express any appreciation you might feel for this capability for choice and change that you have been given ... and for being able to identify and use the strengths you have within you ... and for being able to use your imagination in this powerful way ...

And when you are ready, allow all the images to fade and go back where they came from ... knowing that these qualities you have chosen come back with you into your daily life ... and are available to you at any time ... and knowing that you have many other qualities and strengths that you can draw on when you need them ...

And when you're ready, gently bring your attention back to the room around you and to the current time and place in the outer world ... and bring back with you anything that seems important or interesting to bring back ... including any feelings of comfort, relaxation, strength, or the particular qualities you have chosen to feel and use ...

And when your attention is all the way back in the outer world ... gently stretch and open your eyes, bringing back whatever is important to bring back ... coming all the way back, fully awake and fully alert.

And take a few minutes to write or draw about your experience.

Reviewing Best Quality Imagery

What quality or qualities did you choose to focus on?

Were you able to recall a time when you experienced this quality?

Did you imagine someone else who embodies it, or did you simply imagine what it would be like if you experienced this quality?

What situation did you want to bring more of these qualities into?

As you experienced more of the qualities you chose,
did you imagine being different in relation to that situation?

If so, what difference did you notice?

Are there other qualities that would also help you in
that situation?

Did you feel that any particular suggestion was most
useful in helping you feel the chosen quality or qualities
within you? Recalling having it before? Bringing it into
you from another person or image? Noticing your body
posture? Your facial expression? Voice? If one sense made
the experience more powerful, be sure to concentrate on
that sense whenever you use this method.

Do you have any questions about your experience or
about the process?

Remember you can share your experiences, read
about the experiences of others, or find more support at
www.worrysolution.com.

OTHER USES OF BEST QUALITY IMAGERY

In what other situations can you imagine yourself using Best
Quality imagery? Can you imagine using it to generate more
creativity to help solve a problem, or to get inspiration for writing, painting, music, decorating, or other creative activities?
Can you imagine using it to bolster your confidence before
giving a presentation or performance? To get you focused for
a race or a competitive event? To put you in a great frame of
mind for a party or social evening? To center yourself and let

you be your best when you go into an interview or on a date? To help bring patience and compassion into a difficult family discussion? Many people have told me that, with the possible exception of the Inner Wisdom meditation, this imagery technique may be the one with the widest range of uses of them all.

Best Quality imagery is a simple yet highly effective technique that helps you shift your focus from how you *don't* want to be to how you *do* want to be. It can help you present yourself in any situation with the qualities you value most, and can provide the motivation and energy you need to become the best you can be and create the kind of life you'd like to live.

11. Beyond Worry

*The one thing you can't take away from me is the way
I choose to respond to what you do to me. The last of
one's freedoms is to choose one's attitude in
any given circumstance.*

—VIKTOR FRANKL

The Worry Solution is ultimately about freedom and choice. It's about using the gifts you've been given as a human—your birthright intelligences—to live the fullest, freest, most fulfilled life you can.

Some people think that our brains and minds create our entire reality, while others feel that we are no freer than any other living thing to make choices and exert our will. Our beliefs about how much we can change ourselves and the world around us are fundamental to the way we live our lives. As Henry Ford said, "Whether you believe you can or can't, you're usually right."

Do you imagine yourself as the sole creator of your reality, a passive recipient of fate, or somewhere in between? There isn't one right answer. You can lead a very fulfilled life anywhere along this spectrum of belief. If you strongly believe that your life is predestined by a higher power, you can lead a life of faith and acceptance. If you feel that what you reap in life is all up to you, you can lead a life of creativity and accomplishment. And if you are like me, you can enjoy life while believing that some things are beyond our control while others are well within its influence.

For what it's worth, I believe that there is a force much bigger than me at work in the universe. That force is a mystery; it is bigger and more complex than I can comprehend, and I am comfortable calling it God. I agree with the great Swiss psychiatrist Carl Jung, who was once asked if he believed in God. His reply was, "Believe? I know there is God! God is my name for all the things I did not myself create that come across my path and get in the way of my carefully developed plans and desires." I am also comfortable calling whatever it is the Great Spirit, the Universe, a Universal Being, a Cosmic Intelligence, or simply the Mystery.

I think it is a mistake and a conceit to believe that our conscious minds create 100 percent of our personal reality. Difficult things routinely enter our lives. And whatever caused those difficult things that you didn't ask for or intend to create needs to be acknowledged and respected, if only because it is older than you, it's bigger than you, and you don't really know what it is trying to do. And, again, it is bigger than you.

My good friend Bruce Victor, the eminent San Francisco psychiatrist, reminded me of a sketch with Mel Brooks as the two-thousand-year-old man, describing his discovery of God and prayer.

Carl Reiner: Were you around before God was discov-
ered?
Mel Brooks: Yeah, a few years . . .
Reiner: Did you worship anything before that?
Brooks: Yeah, there was a guy, Phil . . .
Reiner: Phil? You worshipped a guy named Phil?
Brooks: Yeah, a big guy, Phil. He could hurt you—even
if he just fell on you he could hurt you. So we prayed
to him, "Phil, don't hurt us, Phil. Please, Phil, don't
hurt us."
Reiner: So how did you discover God?
Brooks: One day a lightning bolt came down and hit
Phil on the head, killed him right out. And we said,
"Uh-oh, there's something bigger than Phil . . ."

While this greater force may bring us both good and bad
in life, the way you respond to what life brings clearly creates a
good deal, if not the major part, of your life experience. If you
have faith that whatever life brings you is for the best, you'll
have a very different life experience compared to someone
who believes that the events are simply random, or to someone
who is sure that God or the universe has it in for him.

Your thoughts, beliefs, and attitudes are critical to the quality of your life, and a surprising number of our core beliefs, as
they are called in cognitive therapy, turn out not to be necessarily true. They may just be thoughts that you inherited from
your family, your community, or your culture. That's why it is
so important to be able to become aware of your thoughts, so
that you can modify them if they aren't really true and aren't
serving you well.

Many people have never examined their thoughts and their
self-image, leaving smart people going through life thinking

they are stupid, beautiful people thinking they are ugly, and strong people thinking they are weak. They have these misconceptions because they picked up those identities early in childhood, came to accept them, learned to play the roles attached to them, and then saw everything through those filters. When you put on a pair of colored lenses, the whole world will appear to be shades of that color, and so it is when you see life through filters of beliefs that you don't even know you have on.

When you learn to quiet yourself and observe your thoughts and feelings, you have a chance to consider more deeply who and what you are, drawing on more life experience and wisdom than you had before. You get a chance to choose how you think about things, rather than assuming that things are the way you learned they were before you had the ability to choose. This is the great opportunity in expanding your awareness.

If you believed that you had no choices and no ability to affect your life, you wouldn't be reading this book, so I know that we agree that we have at least some power in life. How much? Who knows? It may just be a little, but that little bit can be very important. I was meditating on this question some years back and I got an image of life as a river. I was traveling down this river in a canoe. Sometimes the river was wide, flat, and slow-moving and I could paddle my canoe downstream, upstream, or across the current with ease. I could jump out and take a swim, and I could even doze off for a while as I floated downstream. I had complete control over where I went and how I got there. In other places, the current became swifter; I could no longer paddle upstream, and it became risky and difficult to try to cross the current. In those places I had to pay closer attention to keeping my balance and aligning my boat with the flow of the powerful river around me. Then there were the rapids, where the water raged and twisted its way between dangerous boulders and canyon walls. In the rapids I had only a very small amount of control—but the little bit that I had was critical to getting me through safely. The rapids demanded that I stay relaxed and alert, pay extremely close attention, and use my control to avoid the rocks and slip through the narrow passage to safety. Swami Muktananda, a wise man from the East, once said, "We have very little control in life, maybe 2 percent, but that 2 percent can be really important!"

The most fundamental choices we have are where we place our attention and how we interpret the information we get about the world. These two choices are the difference between living consciously and living unconsciously. The artist and writer Ashleigh Brilliant, who calls himself an epigrammatist, sums up our position when he says, "Due to circumstances beyond my control, I am master of my fate, and captain of my soul."

While the Worry Solution won't eliminate all pain and suffering, it will eliminate unnecessary suffering that you may have been creating for yourself by being unaware of how your brain and mind work. You may not have realized that your worrying had become a habit, or that you can change mental habits. The most effective way to change a habit is by developing a new habit that, when practiced, takes the place of the old habit, eventually grooving new pathways in the brain.

Practice Makes Perfect . . . or at Least Better

Sometimes, if you are fortunate, blessed, or highly stressed, you change suddenly through an epiphany, a lightning bolt of enlightenment that can instantaneously and permanently change the way you think and live. But while you are waiting for an epiphany, you might as well practice the new skills you are learning. They will change you more gradually than an epiphany, but they *will* change you.

You don't need to be perfect to worry well, and you don't need to wait until you've practiced for thousands of hours before you experience benefits. Brain researchers find that nerve cells begin to forge new connections within days of a person learning a new skill. I hope you have already benefited from what you've learned in these pages, and as you make these skills a regular part of your day, you will benefit even more.

In my Worry Solution classes, I've noticed that different aspects of the program help different people at different times. Almost everybody finds it helpful to relax and to write down and sort out worries. People who worry a lot about things they can't do anything about rank Positive Worry imagery as highly effective, while those who have long lists of things to be done favor the Effective Action process. Many find that Inner Wisdom and Best Quality imagery are the most helpful of all. You now have a well-equipped mental and emotional toolbox for dealing with worry and going beyond it. The effectiveness of the imagery-based techniques in your toolbox will greatly improve with practice and repetition. The more you use them, the easier and more natural they become, and you will find that you are able to choose and use the tools that are most appropriate for your circumstances.

People often feel different the very first time they learn that they can relax—perhaps because they realize they're not as helpless as they previously thought. I routinely see that people benefit from even a little bit of relaxation and imagery, but the more you use them the greater the benefit.

When I introduce my patients to relaxation and imagery, I recommend that they practice whatever relaxation and imagery technique they like best twice a day for three weeks. While brain researchers find that new neural pathways are created within hours or days of practicing a new skill, three weeks of regular practice will begin to lay down a network of brain pathways that begins to make the practice easier and more effective. The patients that do frequent early practice typically get more benefit than they expected; they feel more relaxed, less stressed, and more in control. Physical symptoms often disappear. Even when they miss a session or two, the benefits are clear.

People often ask me if I am a regular meditator. I aim to find time on most days to relax and open my mind to anything that my wiser brain wants me to know. In times of greater stress, I try to relax more often, to calm the parts of me that get frightened and allow room for the bigger, wiser, calmer parts of me to pitch in. I encourage you to do likewise—it will help you handle whatever comes your way.

Thanks to my experience with various forms of relaxation and meditation, I am usually relatively calm, although not in all circumstances. I'm not sure that round-the-clock calmness is even the goal, because the things that push our emotional buttons tells us what's really important to us. Using imagery to explore our reactions and to draw on the wisdom of our emotional/intuitive brains can bring us greater awareness, increased understanding, and the ability to resolve issues that can be resolved. It can also help us better come to terms with issues that we are not able to rectify.

The Worry Solution approach may not eradicate all your stress, but it should help you avoid getting stressed and upset by things that don't have to be stressful and upsetting. It will also teach you healthier and more effective ways to cope with the stress and suffering that are unavoidable.

Here we are with our struggles, our issues, and our challenges, but also with our strengths, our creativity, our imagination, our will, and our ability to make choices. Let's learn to use these gifts well and make our world a better place for all of us.

RESOURCES

Audio Recordings

www.worrysolution.com

- Guided imagery audios by Dr. Rossman of all the meditations in *The Worry Solution* via download or on CD
- Discussion forums—share your experiences and those of others
- Monthly meditations
- Workshop videos . . . and more

www.thehealingmind.org

Books and guided imagery audios by Dr. Rossman, Kenneth Pelletier, Ph.D., and Jeanne Achterberg for self-healing, pain relief, better sleep, preparing for medical and surgical procedures, coping with cancer, and more.

Books

For improving brain health

The Ultramind Solution, Mark Hyman, M.D. (Scribner, 2008)

Change Your Brain, Change Your Life, Daniel Amen, M.D. (Three Rivers Press, 1999)

The Better Brain Book, David Perlmutter, M.D. (Riverhead, 2005)

For improving your mind

     Mindsight, Daniel J. Siegel, M.D. (Bantam, 2010)
     Buddha's Brain, Rick Hanson, Ph.D. (New Harbinger, 2009)
     Healing Anxiety and Depression, Daniel Amen, M.D. (Putnam, 2003)
     The Anxiety and Phobia Workbook, 4th ed. Edmund Bourne, Ph.D.
(New Harbinger, 2005)
     Emotional Intelligence, Daniel Goleman (Bantam, 1997)
     Emotional Freedom, Judith Orloff, M.D. (Harmony, 2009)
     The Worry Cure, Robert L. Leahy, Ph.D. (Three Rivers, 2006)
     The HeartMath Solution, Doc Lew Childre and Howard Martin
(HarperOne, 2000)

About the brain and neuroplasticity

     The Brain That Changes Itself, Norman Doidge, M.D. (Penguin,
2007)
     The Mind and the Brain, Jeffrey M. Schwartz, M.D., and Sharon
Begley (Harper Perennial, 2003)
     How God Changes Your Brain, Andrew Newberg, M.D., and Mark
Waldman (Ballantine, 2009)

MULTIMEDIA

     The Healthy Brain Kit, Andrew Weil, M.D. (Sounds True, 2007)

THE WORRY SOLUTION WEBSITE
www.worrysolution.com

Dr. Rossman is known for his soothing voice and his ability to lead people into deep states of relaxation where guided imagery has its most powerful effects. His audio recordings of the relaxation and imagery exercises in this book are available at www.worrysolution.com.

We'll have both audio CDs and downloads to support your ability to use all the techniques you've read about in the book.

Subscribe to Dr. Rossman's blog, read reviews and commentaries, and share with others who are using The Worry Solution program to change the way they live.

Worrysolution.com will help you turn the skills you've learned into your new automatic responses to worry and stress—and free your mind to resolve problems instead of creating them!

If you have benefited from The Worry Solution, or want to learn more about using your mind effectively to relieve worry, anxiety, and stress, come visit www.worrysolution.com.

THE HEALING MIND
www.thehealingmind.org

*Guided imagery gets the green light because
it's an important tool in treating a variety of
health problems. It provides benefits and it poses
virtually no risk.*

—THE MAYO CLINIC GUIDE TO ALTERNATIVE

MEDICINE 2007

Guided imagery is not only useful for reducing worry, anxiety, and stress but for helping to stimulate mental and physical healing responses in a wide variety of conditions.

Dr. Rossman and his colleagues, Kenneth Pelletier, Ph.D., M.D., Jeanne Achterberg, Ph.D., and Andrew Weil, M.D., have created a number of guided imagery programs to help you (or your loved ones) use the power of the mind/body connection for:

- Relieving stress
- Relieving pain
- Improving sleep
- Preparing for surgery
- Preparing for childbirth

- Being comfortable at the dentist
- Asthma
- Fibromyalgia
- And more . . .

Visit www.thehealingmind.org to sample the above programs, for free research reviews and articles on imagery and mind/ body medicine, and to learn about or order Dr. Rossman's Home Learning programs, "Guided Imagery for Self-Healing" and "Fighting Cancer from Within."

Books, audio CDs, or downloads to support self-healing.

ACKNOWLEDGMENTS

I owe thanks to many people for helping this book come to life. In the publishing world, I thank Munro Magruder, who first suggested that I write a book that would help relieve anxiety, and my agent, Barbara Lowenstein, of Lowenstein Associates in New York, who steadily guided me through shaping the book proposal, negotiating the contract, and finding the right publisher. I am grateful to Heather Jackson and Diane Salvatore of Random House for championing this project, and to my editors, Lorraine Glennon and Sydny Miner, for painstakingly helping me clarify the text and bring it to life.

Thanks to my friends Donna Simmons, who read an early version of the manuscript and gave me valuable feedback, and Dr. Bruce Victor, whose astute insights and support helped stimulate my thinking and better understand the psyche and the brain.

I am blessed to have many close friends among the professional colleagues who helped support this project from the conceptual stage on, and I am thankful to all of them—Mark Hyman, M.D., Kenneth Pelletier, Ph.D., M.D., Dean Ornish, M.D., Rachel Remen, M.D., David Bresler, Ph.D., Jeanne Achterberg, Ph.D., Emmett Miller, M.D., Jim Gordon, M.D., Len Saputo, M.D., and Pat Hanaway, M.D. A special thanks to Judith Orloff, M.D., Arielle Eckstut, and Marc Stockman for generously sharing their experience and insights about the publishing world and how best to bring a book like this to market.

I am especially indebted to Andrew Weil, M.D., who, in spite of an unimaginable number of demands on his time, agreed to contribute the foreword. Dr. Weil's first book, *The Natural Mind,* was a seminal influence on my thinking about the mind and the brain, and I have the greatest respect for the monumental work he has done since to enlighten us about the nature of medicine and healing. My hat is off to you, Andy, and I am grateful for and honored by your support.

This book is largely based on a series of classes I held over the last couple of years, and I want to thank all the participants who, in their willingness to learn to "worry well," helped clarify the concepts and the techniques that work best. Thanks to Robin Gueth, director of the Stress Management Center of Marin, for generously hosting these classes in her beautiful facility. Special thanks to my office manager, Marie Russo, and to Christine Gloeckner-Grayson, for organizing these classes, and for all the heartfelt support they have given me.

Thanks, as always, to my wife, Mie, for reading, editing, and thinking this through with me—you are smart and wise, and your thinking as well as your love mean more to me than anything. My bright, beautiful daughters, Marisa and Mariel, helped me get to the title and fill me with pride and joy. Love and thanks to my mother, Marion Rossman, and to my brother, Dr. Howard Rossman, for always being in my corner.

Finally, I want to express my heartfelt thanks to David Brogan, a genuinely special friend who has been instrumental in shaping *The Worry Solution,* reviewing it and discussing it with me at every stage, and generously providing wise guidance at every turn. He also plays a mean guitar. Thanks, David, for everything.

INDEX